PRAISE FOR
Real Women Real Stories

In this day and age, we are hungry for authenticity and connection. It seems that, everywhere we turn, people are projecting a perfect life that we just can't emulate. Jennifer's book breaks down these walls, and we find ourselves reflected in its stories of real women. Whether frustrated by mediocrity, engulfed by grief or plagued by poor decisions, the raw storytelling in *Real Women, Real Stories* shows us that we're not alone. With inspirational and challenging words by Jennifer at each story's conclusion, you just might find yourself pulled towards a greater appreciation of yourself, and pushed towards a life you can only now imagine.

SUSIE HOLT
Radio presenter & speaker
lukeandsusie.com

Jennifer's practical compilation of raw, sometimes heart-wrenching, real-life stories leaves you with the hope that no matter what life journey you have taken, there is still the possibility that you are able to live the beautiful life you were created for.

MICHELLE GLASSBROOK
Naturopath & author of recipe book *Tastes of Eden*
flavoursofeden.com

Interesting, engaging, thought-provoking and a real testament to the human spirit, Jennifer Ironside's *Real Women, Real Stories* takes you on a journey of connection with people who have become the heroes of their own lives. It really goes to show that everybody has greatness in them and can overcome anything life throws at them, if they choose to harness that greatness.

NATASHA BUTTLER
Marketing strategist
boostmarketingservices.com.au

In a world filled with Photoshopped lives and unrealistic expectations, women crave groundedness, and this can be found in real stories of real women. Jennifer provides that opportunity in this powerful collection of authentic stories of acceptance, vulnerability and strength. This inspirational book proves to women everywhere that there is beauty in their journeys, no matter how difficult, messy or unconventional they may seem.

JEN GRISWOLD
Author & CEO
missionentrepreneur.com

When we listen to someone's story we are invited to partner with them in their struggles, joys and growth. In *Real Women, Real Stories: Inspiration for surviving the challenges of life*, Jennifer Ironside models how to share someone's story with compassion and insight. Each woman's story speaks powerfully of the importance of listening to each other and being connected to a community of care and purpose.

GAYLE KENT
Chief community life officer, Morling College
morling.edu.au

Real Women
Real Stories

Inspiration for surviving the challenges of life

Jennifer Ironside

First published in 2020 by Jennifer Ironside
jenniferironside.com

© Jennifer Ironside 2020

The moral rights of the author have been asserted.

All rights reserved. Except as permitted under international copyright laws, no part of this book may be reproduced in any form or by any means, be stored in a retrieval system, or be communicated or transmitted in any form or by any means, without prior written permission. All enquiries should be made to the publisher at the above website.

Publishing consultancy and editing: Rich Life by Design | richlifebydesign.com
Interior design and layout: Amy De Wolfe | amydewolfe.com
Author cover photo: Melanie Klaassen | facebook.com/tmphotographyx
Butterfly photo (p193): Enright Photography | enrightphotography.com.au

 A catalogue record for this book is available from the National Library of Australia

ISBN: 9780648770008

DISCLAIMER

The author of this book does not dispense medical, psychological, financial, legal or business advice or prescribe the use of any technique as a form of treatment for associated problems without the advice of a relevant professional, either directly or indirectly. The intent of the author is only to offer information of a general nature to help you improve your life. In the event that you use the information in this book for yourself, the author assumes no responsibility for your actions. The views, thoughts and opinions expressed within this book's stories belong solely to the contributors in question and may not necessarily reflect the views, thoughts and opinions of those mentioned within the stories.

CONTENTS

Dedication 7

The Real Woman Mantra 9

A Message from Jennifer 11

Choices (Jennifer Ironside) 21

The Beginning of Life (Rochelle Iselin) 41

So Damn Lucky (Nilu Kamiss) 65

From Colombia to Australia:
    The Big Leap (Rosa Arias Perez) 83

Surviving & Thriving (Cindy B) 97

Was It Me? (Felicity S) 123

Comfort Zones Are for Sissies! (Sharyn Reid) 141

I'll Do It Myself (Sandra Hubert) 159

Grief-struck (Lisa Rollins) 179

Have a Go – Don't Hold Back! (Lynda Brook) 197

Red Flags (Veronica Rose) 217

Twentieth-Century Arranged Marriage (Jerry Moore) 239

He Giveth More Grace (Norma Ironside) 253

Some Final Words 269

Acknowledgements 271

About Jennifer 273

More than a Vision 275

DEDICATION

To my 'Connections' family – including my Coffee'n'Chats girls in North Queensland. You inspire me to keep showing up and to keep my dreams alive. You have kept me accountable to my vision, and for that I'm eternally grateful to each and every one of you.

The Real Woman Mantra

This book's subtitle is 'inspiration for surviving the challenges of life' – and each story you read will definitely inspire you!

TO HELP MAKE <u>YOUR</u> STORY ONE OF SURVIVAL, I'VE CREATED A TRANSFORMATIVE GIFT FOR YOU.

Head to jenniferironside.com/bookbonus to download a gorgeous poster featuring **The Real Woman Mantra**. Print it off and read it out loud to yourself each morning. Allow its powerful message to infuse your soul and set up your day for authentic success.

NO MATTER WHAT CHALLENGE YOU MAY BE GOING THROUGH NOW, KNOW THAT I AM WITH YOU.

Claim your heart-filled gift here:

JENNIFERIRONSIDE.COM/BOOKBONUS

A Message from Jennifer

Dear precious woman

Welcome to Real Women, Real Stories…

There we were, standing in the church auditorium at the turn of the millennium. Huge New Year's Eve celebrations were in full swing, it had struck midnight, and my brother Nathan's band was playing. In the buzz of the crowded room the idea came to me, clear as the midnight sky – in this new millennium, I would write a book. However, as quickly as the idea came, I pushed it aside. The notion of writing a book seemed crazy. For many years I tried to bury the idea deep within my soul, yet it kept rising to the surface to nag at me. However, I kept ignoring it, telling myself that I was a nobody and no one would want to hear from me. I was in no way ready to write a book. It just wasn't something I could ever see myself doing.

But that all changed about 10 years ago. I was sitting in a café, chatting with a friend while sipping froth from my almond-milk cappuccino (sweetened with a shot of hazelnut syrup, of course). We were talking about our lives, and the lives of women we knew – all of us real women who carried stories of both triumph and pain. It dawned on me that there were so many women with stories about real-life challenges, yet those stories weren't being told and shared. As a result, other women were then thinking they were all alone when they experienced the same challenges. They didn't know the wisdom that had been gained by women who'd gone before them. I realised that I thought about this a lot. Then the penny dropped. My mouth fell open in shock.

MAKING THE CONNECTION

I just knew that this was the book I was meant to write. It was to be a book that gathered together women who had gone through all sorts of incredible challenges. I whipped out my phone and excitedly tapped notes into it, without uttering a word of what I was thinking. Despite that excitement, I was still scared and unsure – I didn't know HOW to write a book! So, I sat on the idea and didn't tell a soul. That is, until a couple of years ago...

So what happened? Well, I moved to Townsville in North Queensland eight years ago, feeling deep down that there was a significant reason for me being there. Five years later, I went through a major transition and began working for myself (something I had long desired), and I decided to start a women's meet-up group called 'Connections'. I wanted it to be a safe space for women to tell their stories. I started to bring along two jars to our 'Coffee'n'Chats' sessions – one labelled 'Celebrating' and the other labelled 'Letting go'. I asked women to take a moment to anonymously write down a celebration from their week (there is so much power in writing down the positives in our lives and we often forget to celebrate them), as well as something they wanted to release that wasn't serving them. They were then to put these in the jars. My goal was for women to leave feeling inspired. Soon, the jars began to fill, and I was asked what I was going to do

A Message from Jennifer

with all of the notes. Before I could even think about it, the words 'write a book' flew out of my mouth.

While the book in your hands isn't based on all of those notes, there we were – I'd spoken the idea out loud for the very first time. I was like, 'OMG! What have I done?' However, the Coffee'n'Chats ladies kept asking me when was I going to start the book, and reminded me often about my dream. They kept me accountable.

BEHIND THE MASK

My purpose for writing this book is to bring together women from all walks of life and to allow them to tell their stories in a safe place. A place where they will not be judged. A place where there is no need to wear a mask. What do I mean by 'wearing a mask'? Well, it's when we don't share our feelings with anyone else – we pretend that everything is fine. We do it to protect ourselves from judgement. However, a story shared is a burden shared. This benefits the storyteller, but it also benefits the person with whom we share – when we enter the lives of other women we can draw inspiration and often find answers to our own questions, and feel a sense of much-needed acceptance and belonging.

Now I must say that while I'm against the wearing of masks, I do realise that they might be needed, at times – especially when our emotional wounds are fresh, bleeding and still oozing. A mask helps ensure we don't vomit our stuff over people prematurely. (Yes, I called it 'vomit' because sometimes we become so caught up in our emotional wounds that we pour them over every poor unsuspecting person we meet – and, seriously, that's just too much!) However, in order to take off our masks slowly and with a feeling of safety, we need to find a supportive landing place where we can talk through our stories and receive help to carry us through to the other side. This is why I started my Connections meet-up group.

While I'd love to join you for an in-person 'Coffee'n'Chats' meet-up wherever you are in the world, I know it's not physically possible – but this book is my way of reaching out to you and providing support, comfort and inspiration. The women in this book have courageously removed their masks and shared their stories, enabling you to believe that you, too, can overcome any adversity in your life. You can recover, and you can thrive! Also, by witnessing the courage of other women sharing their stories so authentically, my hope is that it will inspire you to do the same (in a safe space). Every one of us has a story, *a real story* that is precious and unique in every way – and to not share its truth is to lose out on the support of sisterhood and to deny other women your valuable insight and wisdom.

BEYOND DOUBT

Deciding to actually publish this book was HUGE. How did it all happen? Well, the process I used to make it a reality is one that you can use to make *your* dreams come true, too (all I did was put into practice the steps I outline in my *More than a Vision* program). Without that action, this book wouldn't be sitting in your hands right now.

In 2017 I started a consistent daily practice of living out my **life vision** in my head – previously, I'd been inconsistent about doing this. You might be wondering what a 'life vision' is. Well, it involves creating a picture of the life you want to live. Behind this, though, is your **purpose** – your big 'why'. This comes from knowing who you are and why you were born – what you are here to do. I believe your purpose is pre-ordained. Yes, you can consciously decide what your purpose will be, but I believe that even this decision links back to the core of your heart and soul. Realising your purpose helps to define your life vision.

So, basically, every single day I wrote out the goals I had for my life. Next, I got really bold and courageous. I re-did my vision board (read more about vision boards in my story), and I found myself adding months and years next to each picture – dream deadlines, if you will. Over the following months, I kept writing my goals and also started focusing on my vision board. Little did I know they were becoming a reality inside me.

Because of all the encouragement I received from my Coffee'n'Chats ladies to get on and write my book, I took a deep breath and created a goal for it. Every day I would grab my pen and write out 'Write my book: Real Women, Real Stories'. I added a picture of the book's cover to my vision board, and the date 'May 2020' for its publication. (My mind would say, 'Yeah, not likely,' but I kept writing my goal and looking at the vision board anyway.) I'd see myself speaking, and I'd see women reading the book with tears rolling down their faces as they saw themselves in a certain story. I talked about it frequently at the Coffee'n'Chats meet-up, especially once I got over my initial discomfort.

However, there was a missing piece to the puzzle – or so I thought. I kept asking how was I going to take the actions I wanted to take when I needed more income to support the vision. In the midst of this, I had three 'GlamBabies' (grandbabies) on the way, which meant factoring in the travel, gifts and additional support I wanted to give to my children. While I could have let money concerns throw me off course, I kept focused on my vision and on WHAT I wanted to achieve rather than getting caught up in the HOW and worrying about the details. The more I focused on the 'what' and writing down my goals every day, the closer I came to taking the next audacious leap into action. I trusted that the financial resources required would become available to me.

THE VISION MADE REAL

About 14 months after starting my consistent daily goal-writing practice, I was chatting with my brother and he started telling me about his adventures as an Uber rideshare driver. Suddenly, I had a lightbulb moment. I realised that being a rideshare driver was something I could do to bring in additional income to help support my children as soon-to-be-new parents. (I didn't even consider that it could also create money to fund my book.) Every day I had been visualising the creation of financial resources, saying, 'I have God-inspired, creative million-dollar ideas to fund my life vision'. So, in January 2019 – during major flooding, no less – I took my 'GlamMobile' to the streets of Townsville. I loved every minute of it.

I kept on with the daily writing down of goals and visualising, and by early March 2019... it hit me! With my rideshare work in the GlamMobile, I now had the extra ongoing income to fund my book-writing goal – I just hadn't realised it. Suddenly, I came across a couple of publishers who were interested in working with me on this project (yes, this very book – *Real Women, Real Stories*), and while I didn't yet have the exact plan for it, the ideas were there. By engaging a coach/publisher to support and guide the journey I have turned that vision into a reality. None of this would have happened had I not removed the mask and embraced vulnerability (by sharing my idea), created a vision from my dream, set a goal and started taking action, always paying attention to signs that showed me 'how' it was all going to happen. Honestly, if I'd only ever focused on the 'how' and not implemented the principles I now teach, I may have given up within the first five minutes – which is what most people do!

REAL STORIES

It wasn't long before everything fell into place. As I sat down with my publisher to create a project plan, I had ideas swirling in my head, tears filling my eyes and a nervous excitement permeating every part of my being. When I then started asking women I knew to step forward and share their stories, I often did not know what each story would be about. However, I trusted my intuition. As women started saying 'yes', and as the themes subsequently revealed themselves, I realised that I could not have woven together a more heartwarming and moving group of stories than if I'd handpicked them from a list of known topics. I am absolutely certain that every reader of this book will find a story with which they wholeheartedly relate.

The beautiful, precious, thought-provoking and heartfelt stories shared by the contributors to this book will inspire you to take another step forward, to leap, to run and to never give up on yourself. Rochelle, Nilu, Rosa, Cindy, Felicity, Sharyn, Sandra, Lisa, Lynda, Veronica, Jerry and Norma have each opened up their hearts and lives to encourage you to live a greater life, no matter what you are facing. I've also included my story at the start of our compilation, because I know that part of my purpose is to unmask aspects of my life and to share them with you. (Please note that some of our contributors have used pseudonyms, to protect their identity and those of people in their lives – however, all stories are true.)

At the start of the contributors' stories, in a special section called 'Before we begin…', I introduce each special woman and reveal how I met them. Then, their story is told, and – being that I'm a transformational coach – I couldn't help but add my thoughts every now and then throughout their amazing stories. As mentioned, I've unmasked myself and shared my story first. Flowing on from this, we start with the story of our youngest contributor and then ascend in age, with each story revealing how each precious woman has dealt with challenges in her life. At the end of each chapter is 'A final note...', in which I reflect on the key messages of each story. It's here that I also share practical advice and tools that you can apply to your everyday life. I believe in offering real solutions that will give real results. This is what this book is designed for! As a bonus, our contributors have recorded special messages for you, and these are available by accessing the QR codes at the ends of their chapters.

As you read the stories of these real women, perhaps you will feel as though you are reading your very own story. Perhaps you are currently feeling stuck and as though you are going around in circles. Perhaps you feel there is no way out and that you have no plan. I encourage you to take heart. You can find freedom. You can put an end to the often unspoken pain that women have experienced for century after century. This is your time. It's your season to embrace all of who you are and to truly live your best life. Be inspired by the real women in this book who have overcome incredible challenges, and know that you can do this, too.

Trust me; I'm not just talking about this as if it is some abstract thing. You truly *can* have the authentic, wonderful life you were created to live. In my *More than a Vision* program (details are revealed at morethanavision.com), I have an entire plan to help you do just that. If the idea of embracing a life of satisfaction and purpose lights you up, I would love for you to join me in the program.

A Message from Jennifer

I invite you to let down your mask while you read the truth of each of these stories, and to share *your* truth with a trusted community of women who want to see you soar.

With heartfelt love and gratitude

Jennifer

PS I'd love to connect with you – come and say 'Hi!' via my website or ask to join my exclusive Facebook group:

Website: jenniferironside.com

Facebook: facebook.com/groups/BuildingSuccessHabits

PPS I recommend having a box of tissues and perhaps even a journal by your side while you relax and enjoy these heartfelt stories. Please note that two of the stories may trigger those who have experienced domestic violence, sexual assault, suicidal thoughts, self-harm or substance abuse – trigger warnings have been included at the starts of those stories.

SPECIAL ANNOUNCEMENT!

This book is now available in audio form.

If you'd like to listen to me narrate the following stories while you go for a walk or tidy up around the house, visit audible.com and search for the words 'real women real stories'.

JENNIFER IRONSIDE

CHOICES

White shorts sat baggily around my ankles. I counted the squares of toilet paper I was about to use, careful not to tear off too many sheets. I gazed, glassy-eyed (due to late-night baby feeds), at the torn lino floor of our dingy bathroom and wondered, 'Will life ever be any better than this? Will I always have to be sooo careful about how much toilet paper I use?' Seriously, this was not the life I had planned, not the way I'd imagined it would go. Was counting toilet paper really meant to be how I lived my life?!

That very day I made the decision that things weren't going to stay that way forever. I decided there would be *more* for me and my family. I just didn't know what that 'more' was, and I didn't know how it was going to happen. I just decided it would be so.

In truth, the life I'd planned until that time hadn't actually been planned. I was just living day-to-day with no real picture of the future I wanted. I knew what I didn't want, so that's what I focused on. Interestingly, I've since learnt that the more you focus on something, the more you will get of that particular thing. In my case, I was getting more of the things I didn't want! Needless to say, I was on a journey to nowhere. At that stage I was into my second marriage and that wasn't looking too bright, either.

YOUNG LOVE

I first married at nearly 19 years of age (and my two older brothers also married at age 19). This was because I had been raised to believe that if you wanted to have sex, you needed first to be married – however, my parents felt I was too young and was rushing into things. I had known my husband for only a few months before we became engaged, and the marriage lasted all of two years. I also had it in my head that it was the duty of girls to marry and have children. I'm not suggesting this particular belief was something passed on to me by my family – it was merely the thinking that I had taken on myself. I had been very clever at school but was fiercely independent and also wanted financial independence. So leaving school, getting a job, becoming independent and meeting boys were all very high on my agenda. I had no long-term plans nor any real idea of what I wanted in my life. Those thoughts hadn't even occurred to me.

By the age of 21 I had left my first husband, and I divorced him at 22. I saw myself as a young woman who had failed everyone, especially myself. I was scared to be alone and didn't want to be 'left on the shelf'. I met another man through a work colleague, and we married when I was 24. We decided to start a family, and I gave birth to my eldest son in 1994 when I was 26.

Rolling forward just a few years to 1999, I found myself with four children (one of whom lives in heaven and never graced us fully with his presence – my baby James) and living the single mum life. My eldest son was aged four, my middle son was three, and my baby girl was just 14 months. I was busy being a single mama, but life became very hard for this independent, stubborn young woman! One day would simply roll into the next, uninvited. It was a difficult yet rewarding time.

I never intended becoming a single mum. That certainly wasn't the plan. No one intends getting married, having children and then getting divorced. Remember, though, that my plan was not defined. I was just busy focusing on what I *didn't* want in life.

THE HARDEST YEARS OF ALL

Now, after the ending of my second marriage I may not have been counting toilet-paper squares and gazing at the torn lino anymore, but I was counting every cent I spent of my single parent's pension. I recorded the spending for everything from the one- and two-cent lollies (sweets/candies) I sometimes bought for my children to important things like groceries, rent, clothing, fuel, car maintenance and some of the mortgage from the home I'd left. I had one of those old-time, foolscap gridded exercise books (the ones we used for maths in school) and within it I listed all of my expenses and the money that came in from my pension. Then I recorded everything I actually spent my money on. I knew exactly what I was spending, and I did this month after month. I earnestly calculated how far my weekly fuel budget would take me – I'd ration it to be sure I didn't run out or miss taking the kids to the meeting point to see their dad.

I never intended becoming a single mum. That certainly wasn't the plan. No one intends getting married, having children and then getting divorced.

Choices

Did I enjoy this rigorous discipline? No, but it was necessary if we were to stay above the poverty line. The kids' father had promised child support and we'd had an agreement drawn up; however, this was never enforced or guaranteed. Whenever child support was paid I almost threw a party – it was a huge bonus and a relief, to say the least. When you are a single parent who is the main caregiver of your children, your agreement can indicate that child support is to be paid, but the pension is really the only guarantee you have. So living within your limited means is essential, but definitely not easy.

I was going nowhere. I still had no real picture or plan for the future other than an image society had given me of an idealistic fairytale family life. It seemed as though I was a leper who could now only really have friends who were also single mums. We'd exchange harrowing stories of our experiences and complain about what our ex-partners did or didn't do. The more single-mum friends I had the more I focused on what I didn't have. As a result, anger and feelings of low self-worth would build up inside me. I did have one very special childhood friend who was like a sister to me and who stuck by me, through it all. She was happily married to her sweetheart and still is today – oh, how I wanted that experience!

However, I felt that to 'get that' I had to focus on what I didn't want, so that I would repel or avoid those things. Man, did I have it all backwards. When I kept focusing on what I didn't want, what did I get? Just more of the same, constantly! Being a single mum had a negative stigma about it. I felt as though I was wearing the badge of failure on my forehead, and I used to think that I was now 'tarnished goods for life'. I was overwhelmed and was so 'over' having to be the responsible one. Why did I always have to do the right thing? Surely I could take a day off from that? My thoughts were all about scarcity – I really just wanted to find a man who loved me, loved my kids and would be able to provide for us so that I didn't ever have to go back to counting toilet-paper squares, or writing down every cent of spending in my maths book.

I ALWAYS KNEW...

Although years ago I didn't possess the more-progressive and evolved insight that I now have, I look back and reflect on an amazing routine I created for myself when my kids were young. I started doing it when the kids slept. I would have a nap when they did, and as I drifted off I would play a video recording I'd made of inspirational speakers who had been on TV at 4am. I would listen to these uplifting speakers whenever I could, but I tried to do it every day. If I missed a day, my husband (when we were together) would tell me I was slipping! Well, near enough was never good enough for me. So I would up the ante and start watching and listening to these speakers all day, every day, depending on what the kids and I were doing. This ritual helped me to form different thinking patterns. My family upbringing had also encouraged me to keep my mind open to these types of inspirational speakers.

I knew, even then, that my thoughts were important. Do you know the sayings 'where the mind goes the man (or woman) follows', 'what you think about you bring about' and 'what you focus on will come to fruition'? Do they resonate with you? Remember earlier I told you that I kept focusing on what I didn't want, yet I kept getting the same thing? Are you hearing what I'm putting down?! Even though I knew I shouldn't be thinking negatively, I kept doing it.

Negative patterns had been developing in my life and I hadn't realised. From the outside it looked as though I had it all together as a single mother. I knew all the right things to do and say, but I was surrounded by negativity and remained focused on my past and on my agenda of finding me a man – I thought, 'This will fix everything'. I had a gaping hole in my heart, one the size of a football. And I didn't even know it! It's only later I realised that it's so important to take time to review our lives. Especially if something seems to be continually going wrong. It's then that we can identify patterns of behaviours that can be redirected by making better decisions.

BELIEFS & CHOICES

I had been born into and raised in a loving, God-fearing Christian home – you know, one of those tongue-talking charismatic ones? Even if you're not sure what that is, just know that my parents were very religious in the early years of our family's life. Our values were aligned to biblical beliefs. We went to church every single Sunday – twice, in fact! There was also youth group, singing and choir, all of which I enjoyed. Mum and Dad have said that they were bound by a lot of religious rules when they were raising my brothers and me. However, to me, having faith is not just about having a belief in God and living a Christian life. It is about having an everyday relationship with God. I feel that religion is just a bunch of rules, and in some circles those rules don't mean an awful lot (to say the least). Before I go on, let me explain something – since those early years, my parents have grown in their faith and relationship with God, and they now grasp a greater understanding of His love and what it really means to live that life. They now believe that God isn't someone up there wielding a big stick, so to speak, but is someone full of grace and compassion.

In my teenage years I became lost. I walked away from my family and their beliefs, thinking that I knew better. This started a downward spiral of negative choices, yet all the while I was telling myself that I didn't have a choice. I made certain decisions and I wasn't ready or willing to accept the consequences of them. However, I slowly started to realise that I didn't know better, after all. I'm forever grateful for my amazing family and the values and beliefs instilled in me while I was growing up. My family provided me with a great foundation and a soft place to land, especially when things get really tough.

In life we are given choices. We can go left, we can go right, we can go up or we can go down. I chose to get out of my family of origin in any way I could. When I married young and then divorced at 22, it devastated my family. I cared that I had hurt them, but I was gonna live my life my way, not being governed by rules and what I thought was a dictatorship. (Understanding that my stubbornness was a personality trait meant to be used for good is, in fact, a whole 'nother story.) Then I chose to take on a second marriage and count toilet-paper squares. Yes, I told you I was on a downward spiral, and this tarnished chick wasn't going to be left on the shelf! I was getting good at reinventing myself, or so I thought.

LIFE AS A WORKING MUM

Once my children were older and had started school, I needed something for me. I also really wanted to get off the single-parent pension, even though I was managing well and had learnt the art of sacrifice. I wanted to work school hours, but my previous career in retail management wasn't conducive to single-mum life. It required me to organise after-school and weekend care for my children and this just wasn't viable. So, I decided to upgrade my business skills, and work out how to use a computer and the internet. I bought my first computer (actually, I think my dad helped me to pay for it) and set about learning how to use that contraption. Now, I must tell you, I was one of those people who said, 'I will never use or need a computer or the internet'. Well, I've had to eat my words,

Choices

haven't I? I'm writing this book on my Apple Mac! And think of how much we now use the internet, including for social media. Anyway, I digress...

I put up my hand and started volunteering for various not-for-profit organisations and taught myself computer basics, accounting skills, event coordination, the writing of media and music album releases, and many other administrative tasks. It turns out I was pretty good at office work, even though I couldn't type or do shorthand in high school. (By the way, I'm still a two-fingered typist – I'm sure my publisher wonders why I haven't been getting this book's chapters to her more quickly!) Eventually, I landed a few paid roles and after a couple of years managed to secure employment with a church as an administrator and event coordinator. I also worked at the church coaching single women, and then became a care pastor for women, for a time. I then moved on to working for a large mining contractor group as an accounts administration manager for several years. However, that management position was more than one little ol' single mother of three could handle, self-taught and all, so I went back to the church and working with women.

It seemed I was good at failing in marriage and making the wrong choices when it came to men, so I buried myself in work. Often, this is exactly what we do in life – when we have things at which we continually fail, or in which we feel inadequate, we try to bury those issues and over-achieve in other areas. If you will, stop for a moment with me and consider your life. Are there areas in which you're suffering because you are too afraid to face them? Perhaps there are things at which you are continually failing? By the way – you are actually not a 'failure'. Sometimes we take longer to learn these life lessons. Just keep getting up after each fall, and NEVER GIVE UP!

REFLECTIONS ON LOVE

At the end of my second marriage I had landed safely back in church and started to grow my beliefs and faith in God. I discovered what Christianity meant to me, and those beliefs have guided my life ever since. At that time I was also growing and developing the skills I needed to survive in the world as a single mum, but there was a huge hole in my heart that I kept trying to fill with a man.

Before I married my third husband, I had been a single mum for close to six years. It was a toxic and unhealthy marriage, to say the least, lasting only two years. After this marriage, I was again a single mum for another six years. During this time, I spent a lot of time taking self-development programs and really thinking about what I wanted my future to look like. Who was I? Who did I want to be? What did I want my life to look like? What kind of future did I want for my children? The thing is, I started thinking more deeply about every area of my life (although at this stage I was just 'thinking', not committing to taking action), except for one particular area. Which one do you think it was? Yes, you guessed it, didn't you? It was 'men'! I didn't clearly carve out a vision for my ideal partner. I vaguely knew which qualities they needed to have, and I knew that they needed to love my kids. However, to be really honest with you, I was too scared to identify specifically what I wanted in a man.

There were two reasons for this:

- I was terrified I'd never find that ideal man and would therefore be left on the shelf

and

- I didn't know myself well enough to even determine what I truly wanted in a man – I was all for adapting myself to the man I was attracted to! (This is never a good idea when choosing a man – trust me, I know.)

Over the years, my experiences had embedded and reinforced my 'love life' beliefs, and I knew they needed to be transformed. I worked with some amazing mentors, coaches and counsellors to help me identify patterns, but there was something that was just stuck in my psyche that they couldn't seem to find – and, frankly, neither could I.

When I reflected on the ending of my third marriage, the circumstances were so devastating to me as a woman. They left me really questioning my ability to please a man, and daily I would ask questions such as, 'What is wrong with me? Why do I attract men who are wrong for me? Why am I attracted to those men?' I remember often lying beside my pool at the back of my home and crying my eyes out.

Whenever my three kids headed off to their dad's for the weekend and I was home alone, I chose not to bury myself in spreadsheets and accounts (I was too exhausted to work, anyway). Instead, I went out beside the pool and had a pity party! Now, I love the sun, the water, the sand and the beach – it all calms me beautifully – but in that season of my life I had to bury myself in work and 'doing'; otherwise, I would never have been able to function for my children. So, it was a rare day when I decided to chillax. In fact, on one particular day I *had* to; it was all I could do, other than put myself to bed. (I was so grateful for the amazing home and backyard pool I had at the time in Rosemount, near Nambour in Queensland – but that's another story in itself!)

THE AWAKENING

So, there I was lying beside the pool in my bikini. I was crying very loudly, virtually wailing about my state of affairs and crying out, 'Why me?' I wanted to know why my life had gone to the sh*thouse yet again. *(Um, ah, yes! I'm a lady who doesn't agree that ladies should swear – but, hey, it expressed exactly how I was feeling! Sometimes I even let out the 'f-bomb', but only rarely!)*

Beside me was a personal development book of mine called *Woman, Thou Art Loosed!: Healing the wounds of the past*. I picked it up and was like, 'Well, come on. "Loose" [release] me already – I'm done!' So, I started reading. I read, highlighted and underlined, then read, highlighted and underlined some more – this book was the one that was finally speaking to me. Eventually, exhaustion took over and I fell asleep. (Yes, I fell asleep in the sun – no wonder I've had so many wrinkles to take care of over the past few years! Sleeping in the sun was a frequent occurrence, actually. Anyway, I digress...) I know that while I slept, I dreamt. I don't know what I dreamt about, but when I woke up I suddenly realised what the problem was with my life.

Guess what it was?

The only problem I had was *me*! I was the common denominator in my three marriages, in my slight estrangement from my siblings (that's yet another story) and in my workplace strife (little that there was). Suddenly, I had to turn around the magnifier and look at myself, look inside myself and acknowledge the role I played in my troubles.

Although I had been coaching and mentoring other women about their relationships (through my work with the church and the general community), and advising them on what they should or shouldn't do, I hadn't actually taken my own advice. Go figure!

More than that, though, my poolside dream experience had shown me the huge hole in my heart, and I could feel it. All at once I could see deep down into myself, into the very core of my being. I realised that I didn't believe in myself. I didn't believe I was worthy of more, I didn't believe I was enough just as I was, I didn't believe I belonged, I didn't believe I was acceptable. I didn't believe I could ever be good enough.

I had spent my life making choices based on these beliefs. I could never have written a list of what I wanted in a man, nor could I have taken concrete action towards fulfilling my life vision and purpose. I'd had many ideas and dreams for life but nothing concrete; I was always ready to compromise myself for the values and desires of others.

NO MORE SETTLING

Too often, as women (and even men), we settle. We settle for comfortable, and we settle for near enough is good enough. We truly don't understand all that we already are, and all that we can have and become. I recommend that you take a moment right now to ask yourself whether or not you have short-changed yourself, and whether or not you are settling. I've just poured my guts onto the table here, because I want to show you that if your life feels out of control you can turn it around. However, I didn't just have my 'a-ha' moment and life was all of a sudden peaches and cream. No, I had to get up from lying beside the pool, with all of my self-pity (and sunburn), and decide what I was going to do next. There were choices to make. That day I could've just thought, 'Oh, that was a nice book to read and that was a nice idea in the dream. Oh, I see – it's me. Oh dear, I'm the problem. Oh well, move on'. If I had done that I would still be in the same cycle. No, I had to make a choice to take real-life action steps to recover from this misguided thinking. I had to be really determined to change my thinking and to change my life. What you believe about yourself, in the depths of your core, is exactly what will come to fruition in your life.

I didn't just have my 'a-ha' moment and life was all of a sudden peaches and cream.

Bestselling author, speaker and leadership coach John C Maxwell puts it so well:

Think about what you are thinking about; when you change your thinking your life will change.

BECOMING WHOLE

So began a journey in allowing my heart and wounds to heal, and my belief system to change. I needed to 'sit on the shelf' for as long as it took and simply become my own person. I always believed I was meant to be married, but I needed to sort out my insides first – this would allow me to become a whole person with no gaping holes, and I could then bring that wholeness to a new relationship!

Healing and recovering from trauma, grief, controlling and abusive situations, failed marriages, shame and a hidden low self-worth wasn't able to be done overnight. I made a conscious decision to do it, and I did it on a daily basis.

I had to clarify in my mind a vision for my life – I had to create a picture of my life that included my children, my home, my career, my health and my purpose. I began to hope that any man I met would complement that picture. Not complete it; complement it. That's been the biggest difference in my thinking. I truly believe that defining my core values, and not compromising on them, gave me a solid foundation for making decisions and choices that aligned with my life vision.

It was around this time (about 10 years ago) that I created a vision board, albeit a sketchy one. If you haven't ever heard of the concept of a vision board, know that it's simply a visual representation of your life vision. You can represent goals that are meaningful to you by using a combination of words and pictures, and then placing your vision board where you'll see it every day. When it is constantly in your sight, you are focusing on your goals. Remember: what you focus on, you bring about. (Oh, and don't worry about your board becoming outdated. Vision boards are ever-evolving – they grow as we grow.)

You've heard the saying 'never judge a book by its cover'? Well, in the past, people frequently judged me. They also do it in the present and they will into the future. However, we shouldn't judge a person's life based on surface appearances (we shouldn't judge at all, but as humans we often do), because most people have an inner, secret life that only they can allow to be healed. There is often another story being written under the surface. So often, though, we judge ourselves and also allow others to judge us (and we then act on *their* beliefs) – it's important to know and understand that you and only you are ultimately the writer of your story. Only you can determine what you currently believe about yourself, and then choose to create new beliefs that serve you.

I'm not saying that the things that have happened to me in my life and to you in yours haven't contributed to the people we've become – however, we certainly have the CHOICE to take a different path. You are not powerless to change your life. You *can* change your life. All you have to do is decide to do it, and then make the daily choice to keep doing it – just like I did.

Would I have had the courage to do this on my own, though? Probably not. I had a couple of amazing close friends and a very special mentor, coach and counsellor who all helped me to navigate the path. I surrounded myself with people who understood what needed to happen. They knew the steps to be taken and they helped to keep me accountable for making changes in my thinking and in my actions. These changes were to positively benefit my future, and my children's future.

MY LEGACY

There is so much that I've learned through my life experiences, and these learnings have filtered through many different areas of my life and, in turn, are now helping others. I love to coach, support and encourage other women (the young and not-so-young) to live their very best lives. I don't want to be on my deathbed and look back and say, 'I wish I'd believed in myself and in life itself just a little bit more and perhaps I would have achieved my life's vision'. I've made the decision that, no matter the cost, I will fulfil the life vision and purpose for which my life is intended. My motto of 'live to give' will be the legacy that lives on long after I'm gone.

Why, Jennifer, that's a bit of a morbid way to end your story! Well, my story is not ending. This is only just the beginning. Do you remember the decision I made – some 25-plus years ago – when I was counting toilet-paper squares? I decided my life wasn't going to stay that way forever! And it hasn't. Scraping by and living in an unhappy relationship were never going to be part of my story. While I didn't decide exactly what my story was going to look like as I sat on that toilet, I've now learnt so much more. I've made more-positive choices, based on the eternal values of life. Even though I've experienced more hardship, at times, along with relationship conflict, the vision I have written in my heart keeps me moving forward.

IF I CAN DO IT...

My life now is starting to look exactly as I had planned it to be when I defined my life vision. My vision board is becoming real, even if it has developed and grown since that original sketchy version! Needless to say, I now focus on my life vision, and I also focus on *you* as you read this chapter and this book. My hope and prayer for you, no matter where you are in the world and no matter what your life story has been up until now, is that you realise you can change your life. You can live your best life and you can CHOOSE to live out your life vision. You can choose what you focus on.

One of the choices I made to change my life was to get off the single-parent pension; however, that wasn't the only thing I wanted to do. My focus became creating a future in which I had *more* than enough. I wanted to pay cash for a new car I knew I'd need, and I wanted to do it as a single woman – there was that stubborn independence revealing itself, yet again! Once I had the vision clear in my sights and focused on it, it became the drive underpinning every decision I made (although I also created goals other than financial ones, because I knew it was important to take a holistic approach). At times, it seemed impossible to me that a single mum could pay cash for a car and come off the pension, but I knew and believed that I could achieve whatever I set my mind to. Once I focused on my goals, ideas for *how* to achieve them came to me. These are not just words I write – it's a way of life I've lived and am still living!

We often hear so many clichés about living life to the full, being the best, dreaming big and living wild... we have heard it all so often that many of us have grown immune to those messages. Well, I know I did, at least for a season. I heard so much positivity and so many motivational speakers, but I didn't do anything with that information and inspiration. Essentially, I stopped believing that I had choices. I stopped believing that opportunities were waiting for me, and I became stuck. There are way too many dreams buried in the ground, and I didn't want mine to be there, too. Oftentimes all we need to do is head back to the basics, press re-start

Choices

and choose to believe again in ourselves and the future that's available. Once I decided to believe again, I took action, dug out all those clichés and posted them all over my walls, and started focusing on my vision – it was then that doors opened and my dreams started coming to pass.

Look out – when you make the decision to start believing and taking action, your dreams will start becoming real, just as they have for me! I've also coached women and seen so many of them move from being from stuck to unstuck. They've gone from merely having a dream to actually living that dream. If I can do it, and other women around the world can do it, you can, too.

If you would like to know the exact steps I used to change my beliefs, I share everything with you in my *More than a Vision* program. Head here to check it out: morethanavision.com.

ROCHELLE ISELIN

THE BEGINNING OF LIFE

Before we begin...

The following story is compelling, and it could be life-changing for you or someone you know. I've known this young and beautiful woman since conception. Rochelle Elyse Iselin is my fourth child and my only daughter, the baby of my immediate family.

Rochelle's story really takes me back, and reliving it feels like a 'full circle' moment for me. I remember when I was around 20 weeks' pregnant, walking around the block near our home in Elimbah, just north of Brisbane. My hand was over my womb and I was hoping and praying for this little person. A small voice came to me and whispered in my thoughts, 'It's a girl. Her name will be Rochelle Elyse'. I also knew that we would always be unusually close. Long before she was born I'd had an amazing sense of knowing her. Having lost my previous baby, James, at 20 weeks' gestation, I fervently prayed that the length of Rochelle's cord was perfect – unlike James' cord (which had been exceptionally long and knotted and had possibly caused his death). When she was born, the first thing

I heard a nurse say was, 'It's a girl, and look at that – the cord is just the right length'. Everything I'd hoped and prayed for her had come to pass. Read on now for the telling of a small part of her story, that of her becoming a first-time mother (and with it happening earlier than any of us would have planned).

Rochelle's story

'What will I do? What will everyone think?' Rochelle was sitting on the toilet, holding the pregnancy test. Time seemed to have moved slowly while she waited for the results. It was positive – clear as day. So many things were running through her mind. 'Is this really happening to me?' Rochelle wondered. She walked out and placed the pregnancy test on the dining room table. Christian, her partner, was sitting in the lounge room, watching the latest news on TV. They had been housesitting together for a few months, trying out the concept of living together, but starting a family would be a whole new level of commitment. She went over to the lounge room and sat down. She looked at him, and he looked back at her. She didn't even have to say a word: he knew.

He knew that in that moment, right then and there, their whole world was about to change. Rochelle burst into tears, feeling so many emotions: nervousness, excitement, fear, shock. She was feeling nearly every emotion you could possibly think of. She curled up into a little ball next to Christian as he comforted her. As she looked up at him, all she could see on

The Beginning of Life

his face was excitement. He was so excited for what was to come – all the highs and the lows. He looked at the bigger picture and she admired that. This was the beginning of life, the next chapter of their lives. She asked herself, 'Are we ready?' Rochelle is 22 years of age and this is her story.

YOUNG LOVE

Rochelle met Christian in 2014 at a youth-group bonfire. He was the cousin of one of her best friends. Although she thought he was cute and had a cheeky smile, she wasn't interested in him. Nearly every other girl at youth group raved about him, as he was the only good-looking guy of their age there – however, this just put her off. They saw each other a couple more times at youth group, and about 18 months later they ran into each other at a pub. Christian was at the bar getting a drink with his mates as she walked by. Rochelle yelled out, 'Christian! How are you?' and gave him a massive hug. It was very brief, just a passing-by conversation, and that was that.

However, later that year, on Saturday 22 October, Rochelle headed out for a big night on the town with one of her friends (Christian's other cousin). It was nothing short of a wild night – lots of drinking (too much drinking), dancing, singing, talking to strangers, losing their friends in the mosh pit and floating from one club to the next. Before lockout, they landed in the last club: 'The Bank'. Lo and behold, there was Christian, dancing away without a care in the world. By this time Rochelle's friend was wanting to leave, so she said to Christian, 'Can you please look out for Rochelle and make sure she gets home safely?' He agreed to do that. Rochelle was now beyond 'tipsy', and everything she had felt about this guy when they'd first met went completely out the window. They were having a good time dancing together, and chatting away. Rochelle says, 'I'm a very happy-go-lucky kind of girl – I've always been that way'.

So, one thing led to another… and in the middle of the dance floor, she kissed him. He kissed her back. She wasn't even thinking. They just kept dancing. When the night came to an end, she caught a taxi back to her place (clearly my GlamMobile wasn't in service back then!), and brought Christian and his cousin Darius back for kick-ons (continuing the party). However, when they got to the front door, Rochelle realised she had left her keys at her friend's place. She and Christian ended up sitting at the back of the house on the gravel, listening to music and talking. As the sun started to come up, they moved into Rochelle's old green Toyota Avalon and kept chatting while they waited for someone to pick them up.

After making it back to her friend's house, a little sleep was in order. They then spent the day watching movies, chatting and getting to know each other more. It felt so surreal to Rochelle that this was actually happening. Rochelle thought to herself, 'This is either going to be a one-off fling, or this is it'. She wasn't sure what Christian was thinking about it all, but she tried just to go with the flow. She was so excited – when they talked, she got butterflies, and it just felt so right. She says, 'I'm even getting butterflies right now, just thinking back on all these memories'. As the day drew on and it was getting to be late in the evening, they knew it was time to part ways (as they both had to get up for work in the morning), so they exchanged numbers.

For the entire drive home she couldn't stop thinking about him and the time they'd shared together. It didn't feel real. 'Did this really just happen?' she kept asking herself. They started texting each other non-stop, and over the next week they went on a few dates – an ice-cream date on the Strand foreshore, bowling with Christian's family, and going to the movies. I met Christian early on, when Rochelle invited him to a family barbecue. As a mum, you always have mixed feelings when your daughter (or son) tells you about a new love interest. Christian seemed like a nice guy, yet I hoped and prayed that Rochelle's heart wouldn't be broken (all while sharing in the excitement with her).

GETTING SERIOUS

On Friday 28 October, six days after that big night, they were driving to a football field to watch Christian's brother play. All of a sudden, Christian asked, 'So what are we?' Rochelle was taken aback, but at the same time thought it was a reasonable question. He said, 'As in, are we boyfriend and girlfriend, or…?' She said, 'Hmm, well yeah, I guess we are'. Reflecting on it now, she says, 'It definitely wasn't romantic or how I expected it to go'. She thought to herself, 'Is this moving too fast? It's only been a week!' It was all so new to her, and she didn't know if there were rules or timeframes to follow. So, again, she just went with the flow. 'Going with the flow' became a thing for her, but it's not something that she'd recommend doing all the time or using to direct your life. As you'll see later in Rochelle's story, letting yourself drift and doing things without thinking can lead you to situations that aren't always best for you.

Their relationship blossomed, and they had lots of fun together. They liked to be adventurous, and would go on little vacations to places such as Airlie Beach, Bowen (Christian's hometown), Magnetic Island, the Sunshine Coast (Rochelle's hometown) and around their beautiful city of Townsville. They also liked to go out and party (well, maybe too much partying) and have fun with their friends. However, Rochelle says, 'It wasn't all peaches and cream; it wasn't the fairytale that I expected or hoped for. It was full of highs and lows and real-life bumps. We got into things we shouldn't have gotten into'. Although Rochelle and Christian had vague plans for their

'Going with the flow' became
a thing for her, but it's not
something that she'd recommend
doing all the time
or using to direct your life.

futures, they made the choice to briefly steer off that path and go in a different direction. A direction that would lead them nowhere; a direction that would hurt them and their families.

A POOR CHOICE

What was this change of direction? Well, for a while, they chose to dabble in drugs. This brought them both great shame and put their jobs on the line, as well as their personal safety and their futures. It's not something Rochelle likes to talk about, let alone write about, but it is a part of her story. She says, 'I choose not to live in regret. My life and story is still being created. I have the pen and I'm going to write the best life story that I can'. She believes that we all have choices to make, and even if we go off course we have plenty of ways of bringing our lives back into alignment. She also says, 'If you are reading this and are dabbling in social drugs or something more – or even less – please get help. It's not worth it'. (See page 119 for details of substance abuse support services.)

Christian's parents, Rochelle's dad and I intervened to help them get back on track. Rochelle and Christian never actually broke up, but they did stop seeing each other for a while so that they could clear their heads. They needed to stop and find out who they were as individuals before reuniting. It was hard, but it had to happen. This was a heartbreaking time for me. It took a lot of courage for me to intervene, because I was fearful of losing Rochelle for at least a time. But as a mama, I did what I needed to do, with love!

A FRESH START

Rochelle started studying for a Certificate III in Aged Care (while working two jobs) – it was good for her, and kept her mind busy. Christian worked for a bank and was accepted into university to study primary education. Although Rochelle didn't complete the Certificate III because the training organisation went into liquidation, she was happy to focus only on her jobs. Christian decided that his choice of study was not for him, and that he just wanted to focus on working. They both felt that they were now on the right track for creating a great future.

So there they were, sitting together on the couch within six months of resuming their relationship. Christian was comforting Rochelle, with both of them knowing that their lives were about to change. Rochelle loved just how brave and supportive Christian was at that moment. She says, 'It took a couple of weeks for the news to really sink in. Then came the first doctor's appointment – I was about six weeks' pregnant by then'. The doctor started running tests: checking her weight, drawing blood and asking what seemed to be a never-ending list of questions. 'When was your last period? Do you smoke? Do you take any recreational drugs? Do you drink, and how often? Was this pregnancy planned? Is this your first pregnancy?' Rochelle found it to be exciting *and* nerve-wracking. 'This is really happening! I have a little human inside of me who is half me and half Christian,' she thought. Through all of this, lurking always at the back of her mind, was the question of how they were going to tell everyone. 'I kept putting it off,' Rochelle says. 'I was waiting for the right moment.'

FINDING THE COURAGE

By the eight-week stage, Rochelle and Christian still hadn't told their loved ones about the pregnancy. It was so very hard to be experiencing such an exciting time in their lives yet not feeling able to share it with everyone. They were simply afraid of their responses. Rochelle recalls, 'I was afraid of being rejected. I was afraid of disappointing people'. She worried that she would be judged, because she and Christian had been through that

The Beginning of Life

hard time in their relationship just six months before and were still recovering from it. However, the day came when she felt she had to tell me – she considered me to be her best friend. She couldn't keep it from me any longer. Christian was fully supportive and knew how hard this time had been for her.

I was out with my Connections Coffee'n'Chats group having coffee on the Strand, so Rochelle asked to meet up with me afterwards for lunch. I agreed and was excited to have some mother–daughter time. Rochelle says, 'I was terrified. Little did she know I was about to tell her something that would not only change my and Christian's lives forever, but hers, too'.

Rochelle arrived at the coffee group as we were finishing up, and started walking down the Strand with me. We were trying to work out where to go for lunch, but she was distracted and couldn't stop thinking of what was about to happen. She was trying to appear cool and making sure nothing seemed 'off'. We wound up at a fish and chip kiosk, where we ordered our food and sat down at a cute little table facing the water. It was perfect; we both love the beach. We sat and chatted, catching up on news while waiting for our food. Rochelle was getting so nervous that she could barely talk. She was fighting with herself internally. 'OK – tell her now. There's a pause. Tell her now!' However, she just couldn't get the words out. Then she thought to herself, 'Tell her before the food comes, or you will regret it'. She took a deep breath.

'Ah, Mum... so, um... I have to tell you something. It's pretty important. Please don't get mad,' Rochelle said. She looked at me, not knowing how to say those two words. It was as though her mouth had sealed itself shut. 'You're pregnant?' I asked. 'Ah, yeah. I am,' said Rochelle, looking away. On the inside, she was freaking out, thinking, 'How is she going to react?'

Rochelle finally looked at my face. It was lit up – all I did was smile. Rochelle started to cry. She says, 'I was so happy and relieved to finally tell the most important woman in my life'. I was so excited, and we hugged and cried. 'How far along are you?' I asked. Rochelle told me she was at the eight-week mark, and that she had just had her first scan. I wished she'd told me sooner, and Rochelle did, too. Our food came, and we enjoyed the rest of the afternoon sitting by the beach talking about all things baby. Now that Rochelle had told me and knew she had my full support and love, she felt more at ease about telling everyone else. She still felt nervous about sharing the news with them, but she knew she could do it.

After finally telling me about the baby, Rochelle experienced a real sense of belonging, acceptance and unconditional love. We all crave this feeling, especially when it's given by the person closest to us. Rochelle and Christian then told all of their Townsville friends – they were so happy for them both. Christian told his family also, but that's his story to tell. A few weeks later they headed down to the Sunshine Coast to celebrate Rochelle's pop's 80th birthday, and they shared the news there, too. Again, everyone couldn't have been happier for them. Rochelle also remembers one of the first things I did at this time – I bought a bassinette for her and put it in her bedroom (she was living back at home by then). It was my way of bringing this special, unplanned baby surprise into reality. It was beautiful to have tangible changes like this take place. They were done for Rochelle, but also so that the entire family could start the journey with her (they were just as surprised as Rochelle by this pregnancy!).

THE PREGNANCY ADVENTURE

Overall, Rochelle's pregnancy was relatively easy, especially for a young first-time mother. However, for the first trimester (from about eight to 14 weeks) she had morning sickness. The nausea and vomiting was constant. On these days she still had to drag herself into work. However, she didn't falter in her work attendance and she stayed focused on the big picture. This wasn't altogether easy, because she was a mere 20 years of age and she and Christian had so much growing up to do all at once. She absolutely loved being pregnant, but of course there were days on which she was exhausted and emotional.

The second and third trimesters were Rochelle's favourites, with her body moving on from the morning sickness. She liked progressing past the uncomfortable stage of her body adjusting and expanding to carry another life. Then, when she started seeing the 'baby bump' and feeling the baby move… it was indescribable. Rochelle says, 'It was hard watching my body change every day, and seeing flaws in myself that I hadn't seen before. At the same time, though, it was rewarding, knowing that my baby was getting bigger and bigger, ready to make a grand entrance'.

Rochelle had been living at home with me during this time, and she stayed here until the 28-week stage. This was a good thing, because she really needed my support. However, although it would have been nice for her to stay living here, Christian and Rochelle both knew that they needed their own space when the little one arrived.

NESTING TIME

So, after much searching, Rochelle and Christian found a home for their soon-to-be-three family. I was so relieved to discover that it was in the very area I had prayed it would be – it was on my side of town, and this meant I would be within close reach whenever Rochelle needed me. It was such an exciting time. The young couple faced the challenges of adjusting to living together, and there was also Rochelle's crazy need for everything to be perfect and clean and for the nursery to reflect her love of all things botanical. 'I'm pretty sure I drove Mum and Christian mad with all of my nesting and changing of mind,' says Rochelle. 'But, hey, I had a vision and I wasn't going to settle for anything less!' The nursery came together beautifully, and she had a lot of fun organising it and putting pieces together. She says, 'I'm so happy I got to share that with Christian and my mum'. However, the nursery wasn't the only thing to be done – other jobs included ordering the car seat, buying the pram, preparing the hospital bags and doing all the last-minute baby shopping. She turned 21 around Christmas of 2018, and by the time she finished work on 24 January 2019 (the due date), everything was ready.

Now it was time to wait. Rochelle was booked in for an induction on 4 February, just in case baby wasn't planning on making an appearance within a reasonable amount of time. She knew she didn't want to be induced. She wanted it to be all natural, but if it had to happen, she was OK with that. After finishing work, Rochelle was able to relax and take time for herself and Christian. However, she didn't really relax: 'I scrubbed the house from top to bottom while Christian was at work, then had a little snooze and got back to it, and then did some washing. I couldn't just sit down and twiddle my thumbs'.

On Saturday 26 January, she and Christian headed to the movies to see *Dragon Ball Super*, for one last hurrah (although Rochelle had a little nap during the movie). That night, just before going to bed, she wondered to herself, 'When is this little munchkin going to make their arrival? How will I know when he or she is coming?' As it turns out, she definitely knew when the time came!

CALL THE MIDWIFE

Sharp period-like pains woke her up early on the Sunday morning. She didn't think anything of them, and went back to

The Beginning of Life

sleep. A few hours later she woke again with the same pains. These weren't just the normal aches and pains of pregnancy; something was different. They would come and go, and Rochelle started to realise that this could really be it. She woke Christian and he said, 'What? Really? It's happening? Should we go, or call someone?' Rochelle messaged me, and I told her to call the midwife. The midwife told Rochelle she was definitely in the early stages of labour, and reminded her that if her waters broke or the contractions became unbearable and were three to five minutes apart (lasting more than 30 seconds each), it was time to come in.

Ah... how crazy is it to think that, just the night before, Rochelle had been wondering when she was going to meet her baby? Well, today was the day. She called me and gave me an update. I came over straight away. Rochelle showered, straightened her hair, got dressed and helped Christian pack his bag. They watched movies, and Rochelle paced around the house, jumping up and down when the pain became worse. At about 3pm she thought her waters might have been leaking, so she called the midwife. She was told it would be best for her to come in and be checked out. They packed up the car, just in case they wouldn't be coming back from the hospital, and left at around 4.30pm. In the meantime, I went back to work driving the GlamMobile (rideshare car), knowing that I could drop everything and be there when I was needed. I was so excited – every person I picked up in the GlamMobile heard about my daughter who was about to give birth! All the while, I was wondering how Rochelle and Christian were coping. Wow... my baby was having a baby!

Rochelle and Christian arrived at the hospital and found their way to the birthing suite. By then, the contractions were quite regular and were becoming painful. The doctor and midwife examined Rochelle and baby – everything was looking good, and baby sounded perfect. At this point Rochelle was only 3cm dilated. She rang me and told me it was a false alarm, and that she still had a long way to go. The staff were sending her home. They arrived home at around 7pm, thinking that they had a long haul ahead of them... but they were wrong!

THE HOME STRETCH

Within 20 minutes of arriving home, things became hectic. Contractions became stronger and more frequent. Rochelle would be standing in the kitchen, leaning over the bench trying to eat cereal, yet going through a tsunami wave of contractions. Then she'd be leaning over the couch while trying to catch a glimpse of the movie they were watching, yet she could not sit down. She had to keep moving; it was the only way to get through it. She floated from one room to the next while Christian tried to record how far apart her contractions were. Rochelle would yell out when a contraction was starting and yell again when it was ending; they both got the hang of it after a while. She focused entirely on her breathing and on getting through each contraction. Christian would give her a hug and say, 'Baby, you got this!' She received so many words of encouragement from Christian and lots of 'Rochelle, babe... babe, just breathe'. He was extremely supportive and also knew when to back off.

Having said that, there came a point when Christian started panicking, and kept suggesting that they go to the hospital. Finally, Rochelle realised it was time to go back. She called out to Christian to let him know, saying, 'This baby is coming!' She made one last stop at the toilet before they left, and there was a bloody show (what a sight to see). She called out to Christian to give him a glimpse of what he would be in

The Beginning of Life

for, and he wasn't pleased at all. He called me to let me know that it was time to wrap up work: 'Rochelle is about to have this baby!' I raced back to their house and met them just as they were backing their car onto the road. I yelled out, 'I'll lock up the house and follow you,' but Rochelle and Christian took off – they weren't waiting for anyone!

It was about 9pm by this stage, and raining quite heavily. They stopped at a set of lights and called the midwives to let them know that this was the real deal. They also called Christian's parents to let them know that it was 'showtime' and that they were going to be grandparents very soon. They also called Rochelle's dad and step-mum to let them know. Her dad was all emotional – she could hear it in his voice. He was going to be 'Poppy Kev' for the second time in one month (our son Harrison's wife had just had a baby).

When Rochelle came off the phone, she couldn't stay calm. She was in so much pain, and with every contraction on that 20-minute car ride to hospital she was yelling, 'It hurts so bad!', and would then start crying and laughing. Upon arrival, Rochelle didn't want to make a scene in the emergency department, so they decided to take a leisurely stroll through the entire hospital to get to the birthing suite. It was a stroll punctuated by many stops, because Rochelle was going through contraction after contraction. The nurses buzzed them in, and they met me in the consulting room (I'd finally caught up with them). We were then given clearance to go straight into one of the birthing rooms.

By then it was around 10pm. Rochelle got up onto a bed and the midwives checked her dilation. 'My God almighty,' Rochelle says. 'I was nearly 9cm dilated.' It's lucky that they hadn't left it any later to go to hospital, or she would have been giving birth on the side of the road!

SPECIAL DELIVERY

To create a nice relaxing mood and to help Rochelle ride the contraction waves, Christian put on some music. She got onto all fours and focused only on her breathing, not even thinking about any pain relief. Her waters then broke. She really wanted to get into a bath to have a water birth, but the midwives felt that the baby's heart rate was too high for that. Rochelle says, 'So I jumped in the shower instead, and it was just as relaxing'. By the way, I was there, and she wasn't actually 'jumping' anywhere – although she was way more active than when I gave birth, that's for sure! Christian sat on the toilet and sprayed the shower head up and down Rochelle's back every time she had a contraction. After each contraction had passed, she would turn around and he'd spray the water over the front of her body. They did this for at least an hour.

Then it came time to push. Rochelle felt as though she could have pushed earlier, but she flowed with her body, learning to trust the signs it was giving her. When it felt right, she leaned over the shower rail, with the midwives kneeling down in readiness to catch the baby. She pushed for 18 minutes... and then he arrived! It was 12.22am on 28 January. The midwives passed him up through her legs, and she grabbed him and cried and laughed with joy. Their son had arrived. He weighed a healthy 8lb 9oz and was 51cm long.

Every mother everywhere has her own special story of the birth of her precious bundle of joy. Rochelle says, 'It was the most surreal and amazing experience. I loved giving birth. It was such a positive experience for me'. They named their new little boy 'Carson James' – **C**hristian **a**nd **R**ochelle's **son**.

Christian and I were both there during the entire birth, and we agreed that it was the most amazing experience to watch. Mind you, Christian did a whole lot more than just watch. I thought he was amazing, and I was so proud of the two of them. I had stood back and watched as the baby's head appeared, and I'd been speechless. Rochelle delivered her first baby almost as effortlessly and quickly as I had done when I delivered her, my fourth baby. Watching their baby enter the world, and as the two became three... it was an unbelievable experience.

A BAPTISM OF FIRE

It was time to go home. Being a new mum can be hard at the best of times, but Rochelle had the extra challenge of dealing with extreme weather conditions. Whirlwinds and torrential rains had started the day they arrived home. Carson was born at a time of major flooding in Townsville, the worst flooding in 100 years. Rochelle, Christian and Carson had to be evacuated from their home because the road they lived on had become nearly cut off by floodwaters, and their electricity was also out (which is not a great thing when you're in the middle of a summer heatwave). The first few days of Carson's life are now a complete blur for Rochelle, with her learning to change nappies, breastfeed and understand a crying baby, as well as not being in the comfort of their home and the beautiful nursery she'd so lovingly prepared. The first six weeks of mum life were overwhelmingly difficult, but she wouldn't have changed it for the world.

A NEW LIFE

Since Carson's birth, quite a few things have changed in Rochelle's life. She has her beautiful little family, but there's no more going out and partying or having random and impulsive catch-ups with friends. In fact, for quite a while their friends gave them space to settle into their new life, and it was just Christian, Rochelle, me and Carson. I was grateful to be able to turn my work on and off so that I could be there for my only daughter, whenever I was needed. Rochelle was extremely fortunate to have been eligible for paid maternity leave, but even then they had to watch every penny. Now that the paid leave has ended, money can become really tight. They've had to adjust their spending and learn to budget together for their family (Rochelle and Christian did not always agree on this issue).

Rochelle says, 'As I sit here to write, my baby is all but nine months of age. It has gone way too fast. My baby boy has been earth-side for as long as he was inside of me!' She also says, 'I wouldn't change a day'. Her little boy now has four teeth, is crawling everywhere, is so strong and pulls himself up onto everything. Carson has the most contagious smile and laugh, and he sports Mama Rochelle's little dimple. He loves people, likes to eat sticks and dirt, and loves anything loud, such as a vacuum cleaner or quad bike. He always wakes up happy.

Life has a new meaning now; life knew what Rochelle needed before she did. She says, 'I have ended up exactly where I needed to be. I couldn't be happier. Carson James, you make one of the most difficult jobs in the world that little bit easier. You are my sun, my moon and all of my stars. You have changed my life for the better, my son'. Carson has filled the lives of his parents and our families with so much laughter and happiness. He is adored by both sets of grandparents – Carson is my second 'GlamBaby' (grandbaby) and the first for Christian's parents. We all have so much fun with him.

WORDS FROM THE OTHER SIDE

Rochelle says, 'I spoke earlier in my story about going with the flow… This is such a common theme in many people's lives, no matter their age – but especially for "millennials", as we are so fondly called!' She has mixed feelings about

The Beginning of Life

the concept, pondering, 'When is it a good thing to just go with the flow and when isn't it?' For example, she has no regrets about going with the flow as far as Christian and Carson are concerned, because she is so in love with them both. 'Carson's cheeky smile reminds me often of how I fell in love with his dad and ended up here.' Then again, going with the flow created a lot of pain when she and Christian dabbled in drugs. Despite her confusion, Rochelle realises that she and her little family have the *choice* to plan, or to go with the flow. Should they plan their future? Should they have a vision for their lives? After all, they arrived at this happy point, didn't they? Either way, Rochelle knows that the pen is in her hands – her story is not over and there are many more chapters to be written.

If you're a young woman who has found yourself to be unexpectedly pregnant, Rochelle wants you to know that it's going to be OK. She says, 'If I can do it, so can you'. She understands that an unexpected pregnancy can cause a torrent of concerns and can sometimes result in feeling self-doubt, shame and fear of the unknown (occasionally, these feelings still visit her). However, the truth is that these little humans are never a mistake. This is not the end of your life and you do not have to be alone on this journey.

A final note...

Wow, after telling my daughter's story, I feel so choked up with love and admiration for her. When you're a mum, all you can do is guide, hope and pray and try to set the best example...

Rochelle asks a great question – is it a good or bad thing to 'go with the flow'? The thing is, it's important to go with the flow of life because there is no point in paddling backwards. However, here's the thing: each person has the opportunity to *choose* the flow of their life and to add forethought to the direction in which they want to go (and flow).

Think about it. If you don't have a plan or vision for your life, you may not be creating a life that you really want (and let me assure you that it's entirely possible to 'live in the now' *and* have a plan). What you focus on is what you will have. Know, too, that fulfilment and satisfaction come from choosing a life direction – and knowing what you want your life to look like when you're old and grey.

I heard a story once about two men who were alcoholics. One of the men went to AA and stopped drinking, and kept going to AA for years and years. However, he slowly faded away from feeling that he needed the support of the group… Before he knew it, he was back at the bar, drinking, and was once again an alcoholic.

The other man went to AA (the same group), and he went for years and years as well. The difference is that he chose to create a vision for his life and to surround himself with like-minded people who had a plan. He decided exactly what he wanted to be remembered for in his life, and he focused on this for the rest of his days. Eventually he stopped going to AA because he had a new group of friends, and he had that picture of what he wanted his life to be like. By the time he died, everything that he had envisioned for his life had come to pass – simply because he had chosen to decide what he wanted. He did this rather than just go with the flow!

While some people find it easy to create a vision and then act to create that vision, most of us could do with a hand. There are many people who can help guide you with your choices, including a great friend, a parent or a trusted colleague. However, sometimes it's really helpful to do this work with someone who brings a fresh perspective and has training and skills in this area. For example, I coach women to draw out their vision and determine their future – this means that, rather than just allowing the flow to take them where they (perhaps) don't want to go, *they* are creating the flow for their life. Doesn't that sound amazing? And so empowering? If you'd love to work with me to create a 'deliberate flow' for your life, my *More than a Vision* program would be perfect for you. Head here for all the details: morethanavision.com.

I've even helped Rochelle to create a vision for her beautiful life – when she was pregnant with Carson, she attended my vision board workshop and designed an inspirational board that now sits on her bedroom table. It's the first thing she sees in the morning, and the last thing she sees at night, and it reminds her of what she wants her future to be. Having that vision is so important to her, and as her mum I'm thrilled that she sees the power she truly has – a power we *all* have.

Real Women, Real Stories

a special message from...

ROCHELLE

NILU KAMISS

SO DAMN LUCKY

Before we begin...

I met Nilu in 2018, which is actually not that long ago. I spotted her following my personal Facebook profile, and it appears that our hearts and minds were linked in cyberspace. I joined Nilu's business collaboration group and we met face-to-face via Zoom – oh, the beauty of technology, connecting women from all over the globe. It's so wonderful to know that women are pretty much the same, no matter where we live on this beautiful planet.

I've had the privilege of participating in a few of Nilu's social media group trainings, and have found her to be one of the most generous and caring people one could imagine knowing. She has been such an encouragement to me, empowering me in my life and business. So often we don't understand the power and influence we have. People of all shapes, sizes and ages are watching us, whether it be through social media or in everyday life – women, we are influencers. We are especially influential, in a positive way, when we live with courage. Nilu has an amazing story of courage, following her heart against the odds and without the support of those closest to her. I watch Nilu and continue to be amazed by her courageous life and entrepreneurial skills. Allow her story to inspire you to embrace your future wholeheartedly, to let go of worrying about what others think, and to pursue your dreams – without compromise.

Nilu's story

Throughout her entire childhood Nilu felt that she was so damn lucky. She remembers only having to think of something and her wish would come true. You see, she was the eldest in her family, both as a child and a grandchild. Growing up in Sri Lanka, Nilu was adored by her grandparents, aunties and uncles, and she was looked up to by her cousins.

Now before you start thinking she had an entitled childhood, let us back up a bit. Nilu was always made to feel special. However, her childhood was not all fairytales and rainbows. She grew up amid a civil war where suicide bombings and guerrilla warfare were rife. There was a time in her early teens when she could not attend school because there were bomb threats to civilian establishments, including schools.

Nilu also remembers going through, at the age of nine years, a time of tremendous pain when her father and mother almost divorced. Following this, her mother dipped into extreme depression, but sadly the depression was not a one-time event. Nilu's mother has gone through many cycles of depression and is still on medication today. No one speaks about how instability within a home affects the children involved. Nor how they may be forced to grow up too soon because they do not have the freedom or security to be a child. Nilu's parents eventually got back together because they thought it best for her and her sister. It was a sacrifice on their part, because to make it work they had to forgive a lot of hurt caused by both parties. Nilu's family lived in a culture where single parenthood was not looked upon kindly, and the children of those broken families would, by extension, be perceived as broken. Family life was never perfect after that, though. As an adult, Nilu can understand and appreciate the sacrifice her parents made. I know very well the stigma you feel when you're a single parent, and I also know that most parents make sacrifices of all types to build the best life for their family.

Looking back, Nilu remembers feeling that she would always have the support of her family, and most of that support came from her grandparents. She looks at this now and marvels at her ability to let go and enjoy the life she has since built in a country that is far away from where she started. It is a life with many blessings, but not without its own challenges.

THE PULL OF LOVE

At the age of 22, Nilu did something that not only changed the course of her life, but also how she looked at herself. She fell in love, and decided she was going to pursue her happiness, no matter who she had to distance herself from – including from some who loved her dearly. This was not the only choice that changed her; there were many other challenging decisions made in order to pursue the love she had found.

You see, Nilu and her boyfriend were of different religious faiths, and attached to this was the social and cultural stigma of their relationship. Her boyfriend had been born and raised within a strict Islamic family, and Nilu had a strict upbringing – this was reinforced through her schooling in a convent run by nuns. Added to this was Sri Lanka's ethnic and religious divide. Nilu says, 'I think I could safely say that our relationship was considered taboo'.

Nilu and her boyfriend had been best friends all through college and she remembers how she was questioned and scrutinised during that time. Nilu was always open and forthcoming about their friendship and how much she valued his influence in her life. However, once they finally admitted their feelings for each other, she naturally hid their relationship from her family and friends. This is because she knew how they were going to react. For months she lied to them about why she was doing poorly in school or why she was completely distracted from what she'd committed to do… originally this had been to go to school, get an education and contribute to the family's finances. She could not understand why everyone was so against their friendship because, at her core, Nilu was kind to others and accepting of people (and still is), even with their faults. Yet not everyone thought this way. Her country was, and in many ways remains, torn apart by differences in skin colour, language, religion and culture. There is proof of this in the marginalisation of the Islamic community, the open discrimination that persists, and the attacks that killed over 150 people on Easter Sunday of 2019.

When Nilu and her boyfriend decided to be together, regardless of the objections, and finally broke the news to their families, she was ready for an explosive reaction. But that didn't make it any easier. She remembers getting calls from her cousins, asking why she was choosing to marry outside of her race when, in fact, there were hundreds of eligible men. She remembers thinking, 'Wait a second. I don't look at a person's religion or ethnicity as a requirement for falling in love'. Nilu certainly didn't expect her controversial decision to affect her life's trajectory for years to come.

WHAT'S DONE IS DONE

By the time they announced their engagement, Nilu and her fiancé had already left Sri Lanka and moved to a small town called Thunder Bay in Ontario, Canada. However, despite moving away, they didn't avoid the fallout of their decision. Through finding happiness with the man she loved, Nilu hurt a lot of people who wanted the best for her. It was not easy living with the burden of hurting her parents, even though she knew she deserved to find her own happiness and their objections were not justified. Nilu distanced herself from most of her family, including her parents. She held onto the guilt of doing so, even though she knew she was not doing anything wrong by standing up for her decision. However, she still felt responsible for how they felt. In hindsight, she thinks the guilt was a way of keeping them close. She had yet to learn that no one can ever be responsible for someone else's happiness. Nilu was disappointed that her parents were not willing to be open-minded and understanding, even though she fully expected the reaction she received.

To this day, there are members of her extended family who refuse to speak to her. She has made peace with them in her own mind and has forgiven herself for the pain she caused. She has let go of the need to ask for their blessing and forgiveness. Nilu says, 'I'm not sharing this story with you to get pity, but to merely share the message that the decisions we make in our lives can have unintended consequences. Ones that you may not understand until years or even decades have passed'.

She had yet to learn that no one can ever be responsible for someone else's happiness.

ONWARD & UPWARD

Starting life in a different country, thousands of miles away from everyone she loved and cared about, and with no financial backing, was not an easy feat. But Nilu and her husband were both young and ambitious. They made a plan to finish their studies and make their way to a city that had better career opportunities – and they stuck to that plan. They needed a way to create financial security and a better quality of life. After all, they now also had a little one to think about. Nilu's husband graduated top of his class and landed a great local IT job, despite there not being many opportunities in that field in Thunder Bay. When their first daughter was 16 months of age, Nilu also joined the workforce. They needed to save $10,000 so that they could move to a larger city with more opportunities for their growth. They accomplished this within a year, and moved across the country to Calgary, Alberta. At the time, Calgary was experiencing the height of the oil boom and was therefore a prosperous city.

THE STRUGGLES OF LIFE

At this stage of her life, Nilu started to realise that her wants and dreams had to take a back seat. This was simply because she had grown up and was facing the responsibility of being a parent and provider. However, she came to learn that no matter how hard things were and how helpless she felt, there were always people who came into their lives to help them. For example, when she and her husband decided to get married, they didn't have any money for a wedding and they certainly didn't have the funds to afford a dress. But they had an amazing group of friends who created a small yet beautiful wedding, complete with an actual wedding cake, a dress, a feast, gifts (enough cash to pay their rent for the next month) and a one-night hotel stay. It wasn't a destination wedding with the backdrop of a beach and the waves crashing, which was how she'd envisioned her wedding to be. But it was full of love and laughter. They missed having their families there, but they knew that this had been the choice of their families, not of Nilu and her husband.

Becoming a mother without the support and guidance of her own mother was another hard path she had to walk, and she felt utterly alone. I can only imagine how hard this was for Nilu – I was lucky to have had my mum's support when I was a new mother, and I have been able to be there for my daughter Rochelle as she negotiates life as a new young mum. Nilu had an insanely tough first pregnancy. She was sick for all nine months; there were days when she couldn't walk. She was in and out of the emergency room (being given IV fluids to avoid dehydration), and she was severely anaemic.

Nilu remembers having discussions, towards the end of her pregnancy, about possibly needing to have blood transfusions if her red blood count didn't go up to a certain threshold. She was so lucky that, by some fluke, she was accepted by a midwifery clinic, and the team of midwives assigned to her was nothing short of amazing. They took care of Nilu and her husband as though they were their own family. The midwives were able to connect them with resources to support them through her difficult pregnancy. Nilu was taken in by a First Nations' clinic (she says, 'How they were able to take me on is a mystery to this date'), and at the end of her pregnancy was going in for iron shots every other day. The clinic later took them on as clients and acted as their doctor until they moved away from Thunder Bay.

The post-partum stage was another nightmare.

Some days it was hard for Nilu to find the courage to get out of bed. She went through cycles of depression. She felt she had no one who could relate to her fears and frustrations because none of her friends had children, and most of them were finishing their post-graduate studies. We can feel so alone when those around us are at different stages in life. It's important to plan ahead and create a varied support network <u>now</u> (beyond just one friend or a partner) to sustain you through every season of life.

Nilu's husband didn't understand why she was so upset and distant. He was finding his own footing as a father, and Nilu didn't want to burden him with her struggles. She locked away parts of herself because she couldn't deal with the sadness of not being in contact with her family. Also, she struggled with adapting to her new role of 'mother', of being responsible for a little human who was totally dependent on her. It was a lot to cope with.

The cold winters didn't help. She remembers pushing her daughter in a stroller through the snow, in the bitter cold. They couldn't afford a vehicle, and would take the bus to buy their monthly groceries – with only $100 in hand. They did this for close to four years. Friends stepped in and helped whenever they could. In fact, they met an amazing couple who would drive 40 minutes to come to their apartment and take them grocery shopping, or to doctors' appointments. Those friends had a son who was only a year older than Nilu's daughter, and the children became the best of friends.

Nilu received another blessing – help with learning how to parent. The Canadian health and social services system had a program that allowed for a resource mum to visit them once a week. She was a godsend. She taught Nilu how to take care of her daughter, how to play with her, how to take care of herself and how to cook healthy meals. She also connected Nilu with resources to help her cope with some of the challenges they faced, including access to milk coupons, food baskets, bus tickets and clothing, as well as counselling and parenting programs.

LETTING THE 'HOW' TAKE CARE OF ITSELF

As Nilu went through this journey, she realised that, as much as there was pain, there was also so much to be grateful for. They were all parts of her reality. The suffering was very real, but she didn't have to own it. The path she was assigned was equipped with certain tools and resources such as people and opportunities. Nilu didn't know what she did to deserve or attract these things into her life. They just appeared when she needed them the most. (In life we often need to just ask for WHAT we want and then let the HOW take care of itself.)

For example, there was the time (mentioned earlier) when her friend surprised her with her wedding dress, or when a lake-view subsidised apartment came available a week before her husband was supposed to start school, which made his commute only a 15-minute walk. Or when Nilu was in labour with their second child (their son), and they didn't have anyone with whom to leave their daughter – they met an amazing family who were able to take care of their daughter during Nilu's two trips to the hospital (the first was a false labour). Nilu could go on and on about all of the little miracles that have taken place in her life. She cannot explain them, but they are not coincidences. She says, 'The journey has taught me that I have to let go of trying to control all of the aspects'. (Don't ask 'How?' Ask 'What?')

It took Nilu over a decade to realise that she had been forced to grow up way too fast. However, it was something that she had needed to do. She says, 'We do what we must, but there is always a cost'. For Nilu, it was silencing a part of herself in order to keep moving forward. It was letting go of her youth and accepting a new role as a mum, one with more responsibility than she had ever realised. At no point did she regret any of it, nor did she understand the enormity of it while it was happening. She remembers friends saying to her, 'I don't know how you do it'. She'd think to herself, 'What do you mean? I don't really have a choice. I either do it, or I don't. And I'm making the choice to do it because I want to give my family, my children, the best'. (Don't ask 'How?' Ask 'What?')

However, after years of making little sacrifices over and over, without a single thought or care about her own needs, she realised that she had disconnected from herself. She was a mother of two by this time, and she knew she needed to reconnect to the person who believed that nothing was impossible. To the person who knew that everything she ever needed was only at arm's reach. To the person who loved to laugh and sing. To the girl who loved to travel and explore. To the girl who couldn't get enough of the ocean – the feel of warm sand under her toes, the cool breeze in her face and the sound of the waves... Nilu, we hear you. It is so important to connect to the core of who we are. You are a girl after my own heart!

MIDLIFE PERSPECTIVE

Nilu had had her first baby at age 23 and her second baby at 27, and six years later she had a third pregnancy. This led to the realisation that she had let life beat her down. Yet again, she experienced a tough pregnancy, but it was nowhere near as bad as the first. The first three months were chaotic, but the Universe (or God, if you will) showed Nilu she wasn't alone. Friends stepped up to help with food for her kids and husband. However, there was a raging conflict going on in her head. She had become aware of the changes she had gone through, and of the feelings she had suppressed, and she knew there were pieces of herself that she needed to put back together.

Their world was turned upside down when their littlest – a baby girl – stepped into the picture. She took their hearts and ran away with them. Nilu and her husband truly felt that they had been given another chance to do it all over again, but this time with a higher level of awareness than with both of their other children. Nilu was older, and more mature and patient, and was already familiar with the struggles of motherhood. So, this time she was able to focus on enjoying the experience, rather than fighting the changes.

The most memorable change Nilu made during this time was her decision to start meditating, and giving thanks for everything she came across. This enabled her to shift her perception completely. Nilu gained back her confidence to speak out and was able to share her struggles without the fear of judgement. She forgave herself for the things she regretted, made peace with things she could not change, and let go of trying to constantly take control of what was happening in her life. (Don't ask 'How?' Ask 'What?')

Nilu had moved to Canada as a young woman looking to create a dream with the man she loved, and she had tried to avoid facing the fact that life is sometimes not easy. However, the truth is that life is not about making everything easy. Nilu believes it's not about learning how to escape the struggles and pain. It is about being able to work through times of hardship and still being able to experience the beauty. Both of these things have equally contributed to who Nilu has become today. They have helped her to create a mindset of getting back up and keeping on going. Nilu says, 'We often sit and want to visualise a better life that includes more. More power, more money, more travel, more love, more giving...

more, more, more'. She continues, 'But the truth is that in this moment you have everything you could ever want or need. If you are facing big decisions, just do the best you can. Be kind and generous right now, despite your fears. That is where true happiness resides'. I couldn't agree more, could you?

THE NEXT CHAPTER

Eventually, Nilu's parents accepted her marriage. They have since visited Nilu and her husband and family. Nilu's parents – and, indeed, her husband's parents – still don't always agree with them, but she says, 'We make decisions based on how it may affect our family. Do we always get it right? Probably not! But we are open to learning and growing'.

Nilu believes that her story is by no means over; in fact, in many ways she feels that it is only just beginning. Like all parents, her ultimate goal is happiness for her children, and to give them the type of childhood she felt she didn't have. Her dreams for the next chapter of her life are to travel the world and visit her parents more often. This sounds like an exciting adventure to me! The most important thought Nilu wants to share with you is 'stay strong'. She says, 'Everything has its own time, and nothing is impossible to figure out. You are only as lonely as you want to be in this journey. Open your heart and experience the beauty in this moment. That is all we can ever influence'.

A final note...

I love the beautiful message from Nilu at the end of her story – our stories are not over, and some most certainly are just beginning. No matter where you are in life, no matter the choices you've made in the past or will make in the future, know that you will be able to work out a solution. I believe that, as women (well, this applies to all humans, really), we need to understand that we are accountable for the choices and decisions we make in life. There is no excuse for playing the blame game or living in regret. Don't ask 'How?' Ask 'What?' So often, we limit ourselves by always needing to know how something will happen when all we need do is be clear about what we want.

What a huge decision Nilu made to follow her heart and marry the love of her life. She chose not to be influenced by others, despite the resulting fallout with family and friends. You see, not everyone will understand the vision and dream that you have for your life. Your life vision is unique to you, and often others won't 'get it' – especially those closest to you.

You are given this life, and you are given purpose. What you choose to do with your life determines the level of happiness, success and influence you will have. (What influence are you having? I frequently stop and ask myself this very question. As I mentioned in the introduction to this chapter, we have tremendous influence on others through our words and actions, and we need to decide what type of influencer we are going to be.) Each one of us is uniquely created; we are not all called to follow the same path. We are all called, though, to live our best life and to pursue the purpose that's written in our hearts.

'But Jen!' you may say. 'I have no clue what that is! I don't know what I'm meant to do, and I'm afraid to do anything in case I fail or get it all wrong.' Don't worry! Becoming clear on your purpose is often not very complicated, and it will change according to the seasons of your life. Know also that you can ask all the 'What if?' questions in the world, but if you stay stuck in fear you will end up crippling your imagination and your future. Essentially, when you stop dreaming and imagining, you settle for mediocrity. I'm not OK with 'mediocre'. I'm a girl with a dream and a vision that's so big it scares the heck out of me!

In fact, I'm not willing NOT to pursue my dream and give it a go – therefore, here I am writing my first book, wondering who the hell is going to read it, and thinking, 'Who do I think I am?!' Reader, thank you from the bottom of my heart for contributing to my dream and vision.

If Nilu had asked herself *how* she was going to live her life after making the choice to follow her heart and chase her dreams, do you think she would have had all the answers given to her straight away? Do you think she would have continued making decisions and moving forward, or would she instead have been overwhelmed by the enormity of how it would all be achieved? No, I think that Nilu decided WHAT she wanted her life to look like and then she just went for it (and she is still doing that today!).

When you've decided on your 'what'... go ahead and imagine it, dream it and envision it. (If you would love guidance in discovering your 'what', I invite you to join my transformational *More than a Vision* program. Head here to check it out: morethanavision.com.) Stop asking HOW, and instead take Nilu's advice: 'Open your heart and experience the beauty in this moment'. It really is possible to live a satisfying life that is truly authentic to you, just as Nilu has chosen to do.

Real Women, Real Stories

a special message from...
NILU

ROSA ARIAS PEREZ

FROM COLOMBIA TO AUSTRALIA: THE BIG LEAP

Before we begin...

I can't believe how I met this beautiful woman. It was an amazing encounter – you know, one of those 'meant-to-be' moments? I'd been invited to attend a twilight school fair with my friend Janine, who'd recently said 'yes' to joining me in my skincare business. We were both so excited as we set up her stall. We had our giveaway all ready to roll, and we waited to chat to the many passers-by. Then along came Rosa, her husband and children. I'd never met or seen Rosa before. We chatted, and I invited her to enter the competition for the giveaway. I looked at the name she had written, and I thought there was something vaguely familiar about it. She was also sure she knew me. She said, 'I know you, I watch you, I follow you!' I was thinking, 'What? What are you talking about?!' It was then that I twigged.

'Oh!' I said. 'The Connections group? Is that where you know me from?' It turned out that Rosa wasn't a member of my local coffee meet-up group, but she had found me on

Facebook and had been following my personal profile. She had been religiously tuning in to my Facebook 'Live' videos. Tears welled up in my eyes. When you are growing your business, it takes a lot of courage to push yourself out of your comfort zone and into the limelight. I always wonder if I am having an impact... and then suddenly, unexpectedly, I come face-to-face with someone who really has been impacted by my video presentations and all the hard work that goes into them. I tell you what, it makes it all worthwhile! To be able to connect with Rosa without knowing it, and to find out that I had positively influenced her life – it really was such an amazing and humbling experience. It is such a privilege to be allowed into people's lives, and it's something I don't take for granted!

Our meeting at the school market that night was truly meant to be. Rosa and I both believe it was 'God' (or you might say 'the Universe') who intended us to meet, not that it was just by chance. Once I discovered her remarkable story of bringing her young family from Colombia to Australia, I knew I had to share it with you. Rosa shows how you can face a challenging situation yet find courage and strength that you didn't even know was available to you. I hope it inspires you!

Rosa's story

Rosa and her family have flown over 15,000km from the town of Montelibano in beautiful Colombia to the tropical city of Townsville in Australia, and have been living here for over a year.

The Big Leap

Rosa says, 'We are trusting and believing God that it will be a long stay,' so obviously Townsville has won her heart!

How did it come to be that Rosa landed halfway across the world from her home country? Well, it all started on the day on which she received a phone call from her husband, Carlos. She was at home in Montelibano with their children (now aged 15, 12 and nine years) when Carlos rang to say that he'd been given the opportunity to take the family to Australia for a new position with an Australian mining company – this would be the adventure of a lifetime! Rosa was happy but shocked, and once she came off the phone she went to her room to process the news. Her head was racing with so many thoughts and questions.

For several years Rosa and Carlos had actually had in their hearts the dream of living overseas. They wanted to give their children (and themselves, of course) the opportunity to experience life in a different culture. Rosa says, 'Despite it being something we had dreamt about, it wasn't until God gave us the opportunity that we were able to realise this great change of life'.

However, telling their children the news was an emotional experience. The children expressed joy and curiosity, but they also felt bittersweet at the thought of leaving their friends, school, home and everything that, until now, had been part of the only life they knew. Seeing them cry made Rosa cry. She understood that she had a responsibility to sustain them emotionally. She also knew that the family would grow even stronger from this opportunity, and that they would enjoy and learn from all of the new experiences that were going to come their way. So often we limit ourselves because of a fear of the unknown. What an adventure for Rosa and her family, taking this leap out of their comfort zones. Let's not allow fear to hinder us from embracing opportunities!

MIXED EMOTIONS

Preparing for the trip took time. In fact, it took about nine months (just like a pregnancy!) from when Carlos gave Rosa the news until they had air tickets with a defined date. It wasn't just the timeframe that was like a pregnancy – at first, when they learned that Carlos had been selected, Rosa felt butterflies in her stomach that reminded her of having a baby in her belly. It was like a small inner fire that ignited and announced that nothing would be the same in the future. It was saying that it was time to pack up and leave.

'Saying goodbye to Montelibano brought up a cocktail of emotions,' Rosa says. She had come to live in that hot mining town, located in northern Colombia, about 14 years earlier. When Rosa moved there from Bogotá (the capital city of Colombia), she was newly married, recently graduated from university and with a small baby in her arms. Until then, she had only lived with her parents, so it was in Montelibano that her marriage was cemented, where she and Carlos formed their home and where their two younger children were born. It was where Rosa met wonderful people who marked her life and heart in a very special way – from each one she's learned valuable and treasured teachings. Saying goodbye to all of this heralded the end of an era, yet also the beginning of a new season where they would get to learn new skills and have new experiences.

Telling the news over coffee and prayers to their friends and Rosa's maternity friends, telling the close and not so close, attending farewell dinners... these events all made Rosa realise how much she had grown to love this beautiful place, and that she would always carry her friends in her heart. Rosa also says, 'In leaving Montelibano, my husband and I were in no way the same as when we had arrived. We had grown up, in every possible way'. She believes it was in Montelibano that God formed them, trained them and built the necessary foundations to face the new adventure they would have ahead. Rosa says, 'He is perfect, and his timing is, too'.

A NEW HOME

Reaching the land of the Aussies was a journey of both the physical and the emotional. There were many plane changes and delays, and a missed flight, and on the way there also were happy visits to Rosa's childhood friend and to Disneyland. On the flight from Los Angeles to Brisbane, Rosa struggled to sleep because the plane experienced turbulence and this made her feel uneasy. She had time to think about just how far away she was going to be from Colombia, and she worried that the turbulence meant they would all end up in the Pacific Ocean.

They landed in Townsville in the early hours of the morning, and took a taxi to their hotel. The taxi driver spoke way too fast in his Queensland accent, and Rosa didn't have a clue about what he was saying – there was plenty of 'mate' this and 'mate' that. Rosa thought, 'What is going on here?!' On that very first day they headed to the beach because they wanted to feel the water. They walked along the Strand and read signs warning of stingers and crocodiles, and they thought it strange that you had all this water here to enjoy yet it was too dangerous to do so. The water itself was also cold, which they had not expected – the Caribbean Sea is warm all the time.

On the second day, the mining company provided an assistant to help the family settle in. This person made appointments for them, helped enrol the children into schools, and acted as their interpreter. They also organised classes for improving the family's English.

Jet lag was a feature of their first few days – although they were awake during the day, it took a while for the heaviness in their heads to disappear. Also, although Rosa had done her research about the city's climate, it was much hotter and drier than she'd anticipated. When comparing Townsville to Montelibano, she says, '... the air feels different, the atmosphere has less oxygen, the sun is more exposed and the flavours are different'. Oh, and the flies! They have flies in Latin America, but in Townsville they were on another level. They kept coming into Rosa's home and she just couldn't get used to them – the fly swatter became her best friend. Despite all of the new and unfamiliar experiences she was encountering, she says now, 'You begin to see that nothing will be the same. From my equatorial land to a new land, a new life and new teachings... but the same God. That is the most important thing to me'.

THE LANGUAGE BARRIER

Rosa says, 'Without a doubt the biggest challenge we've had since being here in Australia is learning the new language'. Although English is not entirely unknown to the family, it's indisputably different to have to use it as a daily communication tool than in an academic sense. It is here that the great help of today's technologies is undeniable. Rosa says, 'What would become of us without the translator and the GPS... Hallelujah!'

Rosa is such a thoughtful person, and wanting to express her ideas and thoughts often becomes very frustrating when she is not able to find the right words at the required speed. She often takes advantage of nonverbal cues to help her communicate and to help her understand others – it has been a daily lifesaver. Speaking with the eyes and with hand movements have helped Rosa stay afloat on more than one occasion when her vocabulary or pronunciation fell short.

Rosa says, 'The people here have been generally receptive and respectful and that helps a lot'. However, a Queenslander speaking fast is still a challenge for her! Sometimes she finds it best to just smile and say 'yes' with a nod of the head, even if she has only understood the final word of someone's sentence (and that word is often 'mate').

She likes to think that the language barrier is an opportunity to exercise patience, that elusive and long-awaited character trait that a person wishes was gained instantly, but that life insists we develop! Through the development of patience, Rosa has come to understand that life is like a river – in constant movement, constantly changing, moving at its own speed and with surprising changes of direction... but always with the clear objective of reaching its final destination, the beautiful sea. This is such a gorgeous descriptive perspective on life!

While she acknowledges that the language challenge is helping her to grow and develop, she definitely feels relieved when she encounters someone who speaks Spanish. 'This feeling is amazing!' she says. Also, when Rosa meets fellow Latin Americans, the joy of feeling understood and identified is immediate. She says, 'It's not something I think about often; only when I find myself in that situation. It's just something else to give thanks for'. (I had so hoped to introduce Rosa and her family to my Columbian – and Spanish-speaking – sister-in-law Mary when she and my brother visited Townsville recently – hopefully they will get to meet on their next visit!) She's had the opportunity to represent her culture through dance, and hopes this contributes even just a little to stop the bad (and incorrect) image that people may have had about her country. Rosa wants people to know that Colombia is a place of hardworking, jovial people who want to achieve better things for their future.

Rosa's main goals are to feel at home here in the new place that life has offered her, and to be able to communicate more fluently. She knows that in time all this will come, so the best thing is to have a good attitude and enjoy each day.

GROWING THROUGH THE CHALLENGES

Rosa has learned so much from the experience of moving across the world. She believes that even if you've done a lot of planning before making a change in your life, 'You're not really as prepared as you initially think you are. Unexpected situations can happen, and you can have feelings that you didn't believe possible or weren't aware were inside of you'. During times of great change, Rosa also believes that we are not in control of all things. Sometimes you may feel that you are not strong enough or brave enough to face challenges, but it is at this time that your inner truths and strength emerge. Rosa also has a strong faith in God, and believes that you are not alone – He is with you at all times. She trusts that, with God, you can face the challenges that accompany opportunity.

When reflecting on her Colombian–Australian adventure, Rosa says, 'As a mother and wife, my challenges are not few; they are many. They include giving my children emotional support, and giving my husband peace of mind so that he can to go to work and give the best of himself without worrying about the house or the children'. She helps the children to accept the changes in their life; she hugs them and cries with them when they remember their friends in Colombia; and she encourages them to face their new life with a good attitude on a day-to-day basis. She also urges them to be themselves, regardless of whether or not other people do not clearly understand what they are trying to express.

When you face so many trials as a newcomer to a foreign country, it can be hard to keep up your spirits. Rosa can't deny that some days her encouragement wanes and she feels tired from being strong all the time. It is at those times that her greatest therapy is to pour out her heart to God. Rosa says, 'I find comfort in praying and crying'. Additionally, she finds it essential to go out and take walks; to write down what

Sometimes you may feel that
you are not strong enough or
brave enough to face challenges,
but it is at this time that your
inner truths and strength emerge.

she feels and thinks; and to call a special friend or a family member who will encourage her and help to raise her spirits. Of course, telling Carlos her feelings is also essential, and she finds comfort in supporting him, too. This is such beautiful advice, regardless of your spiritual beliefs.

LOVING LIFE

When she moved to Townsville, Rosa knew that she wanted to search for opportunities to connect with local people. As mentioned in the introduction to Rosa's story, this is how she met me. It's through Facebook that Rosa learned about the existence of the Connections group. 'Jen's photo gave me the feeling of an interesting woman to meet. A few weeks later I saw her in one of the stands at a school fair. I thought, "That woman – I have seen her somewhere, she is familiar to me". I spoke with Jen and immediately perceived that she is a person willing to talk and help me. I remembered her from Facebook. So, I exchanged information with her, and thus began the relationship that has arisen between us. It was so nice to find someone willing to understand me and help me whenever possible.'

Making new friends and enjoying her new life in Townsville has been a deliberate choice for Rosa. So, too, is having an attitude of gratitude – she believes it is fundamental to life. If we want to be happy, we must learn to see the beauty in all things, in all opportunities, and in all people as well. Understanding this has given Rosa the ability to find a greater peace and to feel motivated enough to develop and complete the daily tasks required for her day-to-day routine. She chooses to enjoy everything she does, no matter how simple: organising her home, cooking for her children, going to the gym each morning, visiting a café, watching TV, doing the shopping, watching the beautiful day through a window, and enjoying the continuous changes in the weather... These things all remind Rosa that life is divided into seasons and that each season brings with it new things. Nothing is permanent in this life. Rosa believes that, '... the only immutable thing is God and His eternal love and companionship'.

She knows that the current season of work and study (English lessons for her, school for her children) will come to a close, so for now she enjoys the season that she is going through. She says, 'I try keeping my mind in the present so as not to be anxious for what comes later'.

Rosa would like to leave you with some loving words of wisdom: 'When you open your heart, you let go of your attachment. You give up the need to be in control of your situations. You become patient and grateful. Your eyes are open to the truth. This is a great opportunity to learn new things – a time for reinventing yourself, and growing up! Life has great things to give you'.

A final note...

Rosa, thank you so much for sharing your story with us. You've given us some amazing, gentle wisdom, and insights into the way in which you view your life and the opportunities given to you. Thank you for reminding us of how to find joy in the simple things that we so often miss, and thank you for sharing your faith and belief in God.

I can only imagine how life has so dramatically changed for Rosa (and her family). She relocated across the globe and settled in a city in which she, at first, only knew Carlos and their children. She also supported her family emotionally. At times, all of this would have been so difficult and overwhelming; however, Rosa has a strong belief in God as the one who carries her through the trials and makes a way forward.

Here are three key points that you could take from Rosa's story:

1. **Preparation** – whenever you face big changes in your life, do all you can to prepare for them because there will always be things that you can't prepare for
2. **Patience** – be patient with yourself and those around you. Every season lasts but for a time. Remember the words 'this, too, shall pass'.
3. **Perseverance** – so often we are all too quick to give up. We lose our mojo, lose our faith and lose our beliefs, and we are overwhelmed by feelings of failing and fear. Just remind yourself of why you made your decision to change. Keep your eye on the vision.

When you combine these three keys – Preparation, Patience and Perseverance – and activate them in your life, there is nothing you can't achieve! Who said life was meant to be easy? Life is not meant to be easy; it's meant to be LIVED. 'Easy' is boring and you certainly don't grow into the person you are meant to be if everything is easy. Challenges lead to opportunities, and in every opportunity you can choose to grow and become all that you are meant to be.

Take courage on your journey and be inspired by Rosa's passionate belief: 'Life has great things to give you'!

a special message from...

ROSA

CINDY B*

* Please note that all names have been changed throughout this story, and that the story features themes of domestic violence, sexual assault, suicidal thoughts, self-harm and substance abuse. If you are triggered by any of the themes shared here I encourage you to access the resources at the story's end.

SURVIVING & THRIVING

Before we begin...

It was on the bow of a P&O cruise ship, with the sun setting and the sail-away party complete, that I met Cindy. However, our meeting wasn't in person – it was through Facebook Messenger! I was a long way across the ocean from her (she lives in Utah), and was sailing the Pacific in celebration of my 50th birthday. Initially, Cindy and I were sharing our direct sales business products and opportunities and I felt compelled to purchase from her. However, I planned on waiting to do that until I arrived home from the cruise. Cindy, on the other hand, was so keen for her skincare that she ordered it almost straight away. Over time, we began to talk more and more often via Messenger. Cindy started following me on Facebook and was very keen to work with me. She joined my Boutique Branding coaching program because she wanted to start building a great business presence online. At that point I didn't know the full extent of her life's experiences; in fact, I knew nothing. However, I did know that Cindy had experienced a whole lot of life and was working on transforming her past into a beautiful future. I came to know her very well, and I am now in awe of her resilience and strength. Allow me to introduce you to Cindy B – she is a 47-year-old wife and mother of three children, and this is her transformational story. Real and raw, to the core.

Cindy's story

Cindy was only three years of age when her father left their family. She had two older brothers, and until that time the children lived with both parents. It was a very difficult separation for them all. By the time Cindy was four, her parents had divorced and her dad had remarried.

Cindy's mother started dating and in 1977 met the man who would become Cindy's stepfather. She recalls that he seemed like the answer to their prayers. 'He was so kind and seemed to make my mother happy. She was finally smiling again.' The stepfather had three sons from his previous marriage. The sons lived with their mother but visited on weekends. As time went on, Cindy grew apart from her biological father. She felt unloved and unwanted and thought he couldn't care less about her. Cindy's stepfather took the place of her dad. 'He always bought me the best of everything,' she reflects.

Cindy's father started to have children with his new wife, who was 17 years younger than him. Wherever they went people thought that her eldest brother and her dad's wife were a couple. This was embarrassing, to say the least. She felt ignored by her dad, and the resulting feelings of hurt, betrayal and loneliness started to become overwhelming. It was obvious that Cindy's stepmother didn't like her or her brothers. Christmas was heartbreaking – it seemed there were so many gifts for Cindy's step-siblings, but not many for Cindy. She was lucky if she received her half-sisters' old dolls and toys. She experienced so many confusing and hurtful feelings of being unwanted and despised, but she tried to push them all down. Her mother told her that her father loved her, but as Cindy grew up, reality began to set in. The man she knew as her father was fading away as he focused on his other family. Cindy would ask herself, 'Why would he want me?' She tried to focus on life with her mother and stepdad, but feelings of hurt and hopelessness would still fill her heart.

THE BATTLEFIELD AT HOME
Unfortunately, life with her stepdad began to deteriorate, and he became very controlling. 'We had so many rules,' Cindy says. 'We weren't allowed to bathe in more than six inches of water. We weren't allowed to take showers.' Her mum would bathe in Cindy's water so they could have 12 inches between them. There was never a lot of hot water because the water heater was kept at a low level. He didn't allow Cindy's mother to have friends or go anywhere, and Cindy and her siblings couldn't spend the night at other people's homes. They lived on seven acres of land, and the children had to walk behind a trailer and pick up any rocks that were bigger than a golf ball. As a young girl, Cindy had to chop wood in the mountains and help split it, stacking it neatly in a row. If chores weren't done correctly, she was beaten.

Their home became like a battlefield (at least, that's how it felt to Cindy) because there was so much emotional and physical abuse. She tried to stay away and be with her friends, and her brothers left home by the time they were 17 years of age. Cindy started drinking alcohol and smoking weed by the time she turned 14, and she used cocaine at 16. 'I was hurting,' she says. 'I felt unloved, lonely and miserable.' She wanted so badly to protect her mum and brothers. Cindy says, 'My heart would race every night when I had to go home. My hands would shake, and I would get sick to my stomach. I would scream at God, "WHY does my beautiful, loving and caring mother have to go through these trials?" It wasn't fair!'

LOOKING FOR LOVE

By age 17 Cindy had been through many relationships. She was always trying to fill the void she felt inside. She once went out with an older guy called Peter, who made her feel loved. She trusted him. One night they were drinking, and she drank too much and passed out. She woke up to find Peter on top of her, having sex with her. She had never had sex before. She was bleeding and feeling so much pain. Cindy started sobbing as she tried to grasp what was happening to her. She tried to scream, to tell him to stop, but she couldn't get the words out. She tried to push him off, but he still wouldn't stop. Cindy says, 'I felt dirty! This is not how my first time was supposed to be'. Her heart sank and she felt so betrayed. She remembers screaming, 'How could you do this to me? I trusted you'. Hot, wet tears rolled down her face. She couldn't catch her breath. Peter looked at her, pulled up his pants and said, 'This isn't going to work. I don't love you,' and started to walk away. She says, 'He had raped me. He had taken the one thing I could never get back'.

Cindy screamed at him, calling him names and begging him not to go. You see, despite feeling betrayed and used, in that very moment she didn't want him to leave. She was so afraid – afraid to be alone, afraid of the future. She blamed herself and thought, 'Did I wear too short of a skirt? Did I say something to make him do this to me?' Cindy didn't feel that she could tell anyone. She was too afraid of what they might think of her. She says, 'I wanted to die. I lost all the love and respect I had had for myself. I started drinking more. I started cutting my arms and legs'. (Wow – at 17 we are so trusting and naïve. How frightening! I'm so sorry that Cindy experienced this, and if you're reading this and you've also been sexually assaulted... I am sending hugs to you.)

Cindy's mother suggested that she see a psychiatrist. She was diagnosed with bi-polar disorder and put on a lot of medication; however, she couldn't drink alcohol with the meds, so she made the decision to stop taking them.

While at high school, Cindy met a guy called Rob, and he treated her really well. She thought he only was being nice because he wanted sex. However, she was wrong. Rob asked her to marry him, and she said yes. For the first time in a long time, Cindy felt positive about life – she stopped drinking so much and got herself an amazing job at a hospital cafeteria. She then decided to go into the medical field as a physician's assistant. 'I thought I had life figured out,' she says.

THE DOWNWARD SPIRAL

Cindy went out drinking one night and met another man. He made her feel like a queen. She told her fiancé Rob that she had met someone new. (To this day, she isn't sure why she wanted to be with someone else.) He looked at her with hurt in his eyes and said, 'If you walk out that door, don't ever come back'. Cindy left Rob and started seeing Rick, the new man. After a while, Rick asked her to marry him and she said yes. They had a beautiful wedding. However, after the wedding her world started to spiral out of control. Rick worked out of state, and she started drinking very heavily. She felt that drinking was her only escape from reality, and it helped numb her feelings of turmoil. She also started gambling, losing thousands and thousands of dollars.

She remembers fighting with Rick one night, and then locking herself in the bedroom and climbing inside the closet. She felt so lost, hurt, empty and worthless, and that Rick didn't love her. Cindy hated who she'd become. Sobbing, she grabbed at the bottle of painkillers in her purse, emptying the bottle into her hand and shoving the pills into her mouth. She gulped down some water and tried to swallow the pills, just as Rick knocked on the door. He came in and said, 'What in the hell are you doing?' He grabbed at her, yelling at her and telling her how stupid she was. He put his fingers in her mouth and started pulling out the pills. Cindy recalls, 'I tried to fight back. I wanted to die. I grabbed a rifle from the closet and wrestled with him. But he won'.

Cindy screamed at Rick, telling him to get out. She wanted to be left alone, so she lied and told him she was OK. He left so that she could calm down. However, she found a razor and began cutting herself. Her reasoning was that the more pain she caused on the outside, the less pain she felt on the inside. Cindy then sat looking out a window, and when she saw Rick return home she grabbed a towel and tried to wipe the blood away. She was a drunken bloody mess. Her whole body felt hot and she could feel the anger building inside of her. When Rick saw her, he called her mother and they admitted her to a psych ward at the hospital where Cindy worked. She was embarrassed and ashamed. They had her on so many pills that she didn't know who she was. Three days later, while she was still in hospital, Rick served her with divorce papers. He knew she couldn't hurt herself there. She says, 'I lost everything. My husband, my job and myself'.

Sobbing, she grabbed at the bottle of painkillers in her purse, emptying the bottle into her hand and shoving the pills into her mouth.

ROCK BOTTOM

Cindy searched madly for anything to numb her pain. She started using methamphetamine, LSD, cocaine and mushrooms, and she continued to cut herself. She met a guy called Noah and started living with him in her car and on the streets, and only showered occasionally. Cindy stayed high and drunk 24 hours a day. She felt angry, unloved, unwanted and betrayed. She recalls, 'I wanted to die. I wondered why everyone I loved left me when I got close to them – what was wrong with me?' She found herself screaming at God, asking him to take her. To let her die. To leave the miserable world she was drowning in. Darkness surrounded her everyday existence. She didn't know how to face reality anymore.

At one stage Cindy got really high and stayed awake for over 20 days. She started hallucinating and thought that Noah was trying to kill her. She drove in the snow for over an hour, leaving behind all of her belongings. She went to a friend's house and asked for new clothes, and gave her friend everything from the car because she felt it was bugged. She then drove to her brother's house and hid in a corner under a blanket. She feared for her life. Her brother and sister-in-law tied her hands and drove her straight to rehab. Cindy didn't want to go. She was angry. However, when she sobered up, she played by the rules. She stayed in a program for 60 days and was then released.

Unfortunately, the stint in rehab didn't create change in Cindy's life. She recalls, 'I went back to using because I felt that this was the only way to feel loved. It was one thing that nobody could take away from me. I didn't want to be sober. I didn't want to feel anything, and things kept happening to give me more reasons to use'. So, the cycle continued, and she started drinking heavily and doing drugs. She ended up becoming pregnant. Cindy didn't want a baby, and she was in no way ready. Her boyfriend, Noah, wanted the baby, and promised they'd stay together and have a good life. Cindy did her best to come to terms with her pregnancy, but having had no real experience with babies (and not knowing how to love or take care of herself), she couldn't bond with baby Dylan when he was born. She just didn't know how to love him. To cope, she started drinking, taking drugs and sleeping around. She and Noah were fighting all the time, and when Dylan was nearly three years of age they decided to break up. With tears streaming down her face, she said goodbye to Dylan and moved out into a small basement apartment.

The shock of leaving her son made Cindy decide that she would get her life together. However, depression surrounded her. Despite this, she kept trying, and finally secured a job – this allowed her to start believing that she really could make it, and could go back to being a mother. But she just couldn't stay away from drugs. In the end, she lost that job. She felt so empty and so alone, and the darkness began to surround her yet again. This time, though, she fell into a deep depression. She didn't want to feel anything – she just wanted to numb the pain. She was again suicidal, and began drinking heavily. Cindy remembers waking up in her apartment alone, with her whole body shaking and her head pounding. She walked around drinking any leftover alcohol she could find.

At this point, she broke down and called her mother, telling her that she was sick and needed a bottle of alcohol. She felt terrible. She had never been so low (or so she thought). Her mother went to a store and bought a bottle for her. Cindy's family was part of the Church of Jesus Christ of Latter-day Saints (LDS) and her mother had never bought any type of alcohol before. Cindy's heart raced and tears streamed down her face as her mother knocked on the door. She couldn't let her see her like that. She felt ashamed and guilty. She opened the window by the door and, with a shaky voice, said, 'Please, just leave it on the step'. Her mother had tears in her eyes as she bent down to do so. Cindy could feel her pain as she walked and then drove away. She says, 'I opened the door and got the bottle. I drank it as quickly as I could and then passed out'.

HEARTBREAK

The next morning, Cindy awoke suddenly to the sound of her phone ringing. It was Noah, Dylan's father. It had only been a few months since she had left her little boy. Noah told her some of the most devastating news she thought she'd ever hear, and while she listened her heart sank and her face felt as though it was on fire. He said that he was moving to the east side of the United States, and he was taking their son and going to live with his mother. Cindy sobbed. She begged him not to take her son. She then dropped the phone and fell to the floor screaming, and asking God, 'When will the pain and trials end?' Hearing the news took Cindy to a fresh low, and she needed to numb the pain so she finished off a bottle of alcohol. She dreaded having to say goodbye to Dylan, and she wanted to fight to keep him near her. But what kind of mother would she be? She had no job; she was an alcoholic and a drug addict who didn't love or care for herself. She loved her son and thought she still loved his dad, but she felt numb.

Two days went by in a complete blur. There was a knock at her door, and she knew it was time to say goodbye to her little boy. It felt as though someone had pushed a knife through her heart. She couldn't speak. She couldn't catch her breath. She was sobbing. At the door was the man and the child she was supposed to make a life with. Cindy wanted her child to have the best in life; however, she also knew she wasn't ready to provide it for him. She began to shake uncontrollably, and she held Dylan so tight. He didn't understand what was happening. She told him how much she loved him and how sorry she was. Noah said that he would get settled and find a job and be back in one year to get her. She agreed to let him take Dylan, even though she didn't really have a choice. Their train was leaving at 4am, so they stayed at Cindy's apartment until it was time to leave. Noah's brother was there, too. They all went to the station together and Cindy watched as the train pulled up. She wanted to grab Dylan and run. But she knew she couldn't do that. She watched as they got in line to board the train, and she couldn't hold back the tears. Dylan said, 'I love you, Mom,' and she promised him they'd be together in a year.

As the train pulled away, Cindy lost it. She felt as though her heart was being ripped out of her chest. She couldn't breathe and she felt as though she was passing out. Noah's brother put her in his truck and drove her back to her apartment. He promised to stay with her to make sure she was OK. Cindy says, 'I felt alone, heartbroken, guilty and so disappointed'. She kept saying over and over again, 'Why?! How could I let this happen? How could I have a son and just let him go?' She felt worthless, and the pain was unbearable. Straight away, Cindy called and got some drugs and made sure she had a bottle of alcohol. She numbed the pain in the only way she knew, and Noah's brother also used some of the drugs. She stopped caring about everyone and everything. She didn't care if she lived or died. Once again, she started living recklessly, falling victim to drugs and going from bar to bar and leaving with different guys.

A NEW LOW

Cindy remembers a time when she blacked out and woke up early in the morning in a strange house. She had no clothes on from the waist down. She was so frightened, and tried to remember what had happened. 'Where am I? Who did I leave with?' She jumped up and worked out that she was alone. She scrambled to find her phone, clothes and purse so that she could call her friend Macy. Cindy felt disgusted and dirty. How could she let this happen again? She knew she'd been raped. She phoned Macy, screaming that she didn't know where she was and that she needed to get out of there. Macy said, 'Go look for a street sign'. Cindy went outside but couldn't see one, so Macy said, 'Go back into the house and look for some mail with an address'. If you're ever in a situation like this, please take close note of where you are and have a potential escape plan (and a fully charged phone). Rely on a network of friends who know where you are and who can be there to help you out. Please share this advice with anyone who could benefit from it.

Cindy ran back to the door, and as she approached it, she got a sick feeling. Flashes of the night before started to come back. She couldn't breathe. She pushed open the door and rushed to find anything that would help her know where she was. Finally, she came across a piece of mail. She rambled off the address and screamed at Macy to hurry. Fear started to consume her. Flashbacks from the night before. Cindy was screaming. It was dark. Someone had had hold of her wrists while someone else raped her. Reality started to set in.

Cindy went outside to wait for Macy. The sun had just begun to shine across the grass, which was dusted with frozen dew. She could feel the blades of grass crunch under her feet, and a cold chill in the air. She sat down and waited. Finally, Macy pulled up. Cindy's feet pounded on the concrete as she ran to the car. She was sobbing. Macy hugged her, and they drove away. Darkness then started to surround her as she remembered the night her son was taken away on the train. Tears ran down her face and the feeling of guilt was overwhelming. She screamed at God, 'Why am I being punished?'

Surviving & Thriving

REUNITED

A year of chaos and pain had gone by, and it was time for Noah to come to get her and fly her back east to reunite with Dylan. However, Cindy had met someone else, and had fallen for him – so, initially, she didn't want to go. She asked herself, 'Do I still love him?' and she worried that she would be far away from all of her family. In the end, though, Cindy decided to go, to see if she could change her life and be a mother to her son.

When Noah arrived to pick her up, she felt as though someone had punched her in the stomach. All of the anger she had been storing up over the year rose to the surface as she stood looking at him. She yelled at him and told him she was worried that she was making a mistake, but he assured her that everything would be OK. She got her things together, and they left for the drive to the airport, which seemed to take forever. The flight was a few hours long, so Cindy eased her anxiety by having a few drinks on the plane. When they landed in Ohio, so many thoughts ran through Cindy's mind during the drive to the house: 'How can I face my child? What will I say? How will things be? Can he ever forgive me?' She was anxious and afraid. Cindy thought, 'How could I have been such a terrible mother?' She hated herself and who she had become.

They pulled into the driveway and Cindy got out of the car. 'Snow was falling on my face and it was so cold,' she says. It was now time. It had been a whole year since she'd seen her son. It was close to Christmas, and she remembers seeing a decorated tree through the front window. Her anxiety grew as she waited for Dylan to be brought out. Tears started to fill her eyes when she saw him. He jumped into her arms, and all Cindy could do was hold onto him and sob and tell him how much she loved him. So many emotions went through her: 'I felt joy, heartache, love and guilt'. She whispered in his ear that she would never leave him again. However, she thought to herself, 'I can't wait to be a mother to my son, but am I ready?'

The next day, Cindy was informed that she couldn't stay home with Dylan and that he would be going to a babysitter. When Noah got off work, he would collect Dylan and bring him home. Cindy was hurt, confused and angry. She says, 'How could I bond with him or be a mother to him?' She wondered why they would bring her all that way, away from her family, and not let her look after Dylan. 'I didn't know anyone there,' she says, '... and I thought my time would be filled with caring for my son'. However, Noah and his mother felt that, as a drug addict, Cindy was not capable of being a mother. They said to her, 'You have to prove to us that you have changed, and that you can be a proper mother. You have to meet our expectations'. Although she knew deep down that they were right, and that Dylan deserved the best care possible, it didn't stop her from feeling rejected. She soon discovered that she was only a couple of blocks away from a bar and, because she wanted to numb her pain, she quickly fell back into her default coping mechanism.

BLOWING HER CHANCE

One day she decided to walk to the bar. She drank until she blacked out, and then she left with a guy in order to continue the party. When she returned to the house, everyone was furious with her. She felt her face start to burn and her anger rise. She screamed at Noah, asking him for answers. He told her he would buy her a bottle of alcohol as long as she would stay out of bars. So she drank, and drank, and drank. She was missing home. She missed her family. One night, after a big drinking session, she yelled at Noah and told him she hated him. 'How could you destroy my life?' she screamed. Dylan was terrified.

Surviving & Thriving

The next day Noah's parents told her they had bought her an airline ticket and were flying her home. They'd decided that it wasn't going to work to have her there. Cindy says, 'I couldn't breathe. I felt sick'. All of the promises she had told her son were now going to be lies. She pleaded for more time, but they told her it was too late. She was devastated. Tears fell from her eyes and stung her cheeks like acid.

On the way to the airport she was trying to think of what to say to Dylan. She'd promised she would never leave him again, yet here she was, walking out on him yet again. She grabbed her luggage and as she approached the gates she turned and faced him. Cindy said, 'Son, I have to go. I'm so, so sorry and I love you very much'. Dylan cried and told her he didn't want her to go. He said, 'Mommy, you promised'. She held him for a minute, and then quickly turned and walked away. She could hear him crying, pleading with her not to go. Her heart was breaking, and she wanted to run back to him. She knew, though, that she'd already caused enough pain and hurt. It was over. Cindy boarded the plane and drank for the entire flight home.

Cindy recalls, 'I felt like a coward. Like a failure. I no longer had any desire to live. I knew the emptiness I felt would destroy me. I had failed as a mother, fiancée, wife, daughter, friend and woman'. Over and over again she asked herself why she couldn't stop the drugs and alcohol – why did she let them control and consume her?

THE DARK SIDE

When Cindy arrived home, she immediately restarted drinking and taking drugs. She went even harder this time, if that was at all possible! She became a very angry and hard person, with no respect for herself or anyone else. Cindy also distanced herself from her family. She ran with gangs and saw more guns, drugs

He said, 'Mommy, you promised'. She held him for a minute, and then quickly turned and walked away. She could hear him crying, pleading with her not to go.

and death than she ever thought possible. She reached into the dark side of life, and didn't care: 'I started dealing drugs hard to support my habit. Meth, cocaine, weed and pills. I went through relationship after relationship, and I was in and out of jail'. Wow, what kind of a life was this for Cindy? If only we could reach back in time and stop the roller-coaster!

During this period of her life, Cindy was sexually, emotionally and physically abused. She lost all hope. She was in complete darkness. She was totally addicted to the drug-taking and drinking lifestyle. To Cindy, people around her were like puppets on a string; she was in control of what anyone did because she had what they wanted – drugs. So, they would steal for her, and she believes they would even have killed for her, if she'd asked them to. Cindy says, 'I had fallen into the depths of hell. I was lost and broken. Who was I? Who was the person I had become?' Cindy had charges against her for DUI (driving under the influence), drug possession, intent to distribute drugs, and domestic violence. She had threatened people's lives and protective orders were issued against her.

All Cindy wanted was someone to love her. She met a guy called Billy and started a relationship with him. He made her believe that he loved her, and that she was his everything. I believe every girl alive wants this! They started dealing a lot of drugs, and he began travelling over state lines. He always took his vehicle, but on one occasion he wanted to take her car and for her to go with him. Cindy says, 'I was scared to death. We had a lot of cash on us, as well as drugs and paraphernalia'. On the journey, she felt tired and nauseous, and the drive seemed to take forever. Her intuition was telling her that something was not right. Her anxiety was overwhelming.

Despite feeling engulfed by a feeling of foreboding, Cindy entered a house with Billy to pick out drugs and try them. Her heart was racing, and her hands were clammy. She noticed guns around, as well as loads of drugs. She didn't think she'd ever seen that many drugs before. Billy chose and tested a batch, and Cindy said to him, 'It looks like it has a lot of cut in it'. However, for some reason that was the batch he wanted. She felt sick. Something wasn't right.

Finally, they started their return journey. Just as they crossed the state line and only about five hours from home, they passed a highway patrol cop who then turned around his motorcycle and switched on his lights. She knew this wasn't going to end well. Billy didn't have a licence, so they searched her car. They only found drug paraphernalia, but they wanted to seize her vehicle to check it further. She was so scared, and sick to her stomach. Cindy had never had this much dope in her vehicle before. She was praying they wouldn't find it. While the police seized the car for the search, Billy and Cindy were taken to jail.

Billy called a bail bondsman and was out within a couple of days, but Cindy remained in jail because her family refused to post bail. She was alone, afraid and miserable. A few days later Billy showed up and bailed her out. The police search of her car had resulted in them finding all of the drugs, so Cindy faced charges and prison time. However, while out on bail, she went right back to using drugs (and selling them to support her addiction). Despite this, Cindy's mum stepped in and hired an attorney to help defend her against the drug-trafficking charges. Cindy went to rehab and served some jail time, yet while she was on probation she met and secretly married a guy called Luke who was running from parole. While serving 30 days in jail for her various charges, she had time to think. She was finally sober and she realised she was tired.

THE TURNAROUND

Cindy was tired of the lifestyle. Tired of running. Tired of hurting people. She was finally *done*. She got out of prison and moved to a place where nobody would find her. She wanted to isolate herself. She turned off her phone. Her new husband Luke was in prison and she was alone. Fighting the urge to call old friends was a constant battle. However, Cindy stayed sober. She started going to church. She wanted to be strong when her husband was released – he served 2½ years and was then released. They decided to have a child, and Cindy had a son in 2012.

She was desperate for things to be different this time. She knew she could bond with her son and be a good mother. Her heart broke each time she thought of her eldest son. All she could do was keep praying that one day he would forgive her, and hope that he would understand that his mother had been sick. Cindy's brother built a new home and let them move into it and rent it. In 2016 they had a daughter. Luke is 10 years younger than Cindy, and she is an older mother. However, she says, 'I couldn't have been more blessed to have them. We now have a beautiful home and two gorgeous kids'.

Cindy had a couple of very positive influences – she chose to reconnect with her family's faith (the Church of Jesus Christ of Latter-day Saints) and to join a direct sales company. She says, 'Through the business, I met an amazing woman who became my life coach. She has taught me so much and helped me to grow and to find my self-worth'. (By the way, that life coach would be me! It has been an honour to be part of Cindy's incredible journey.) Staying positive is a choice Cindy makes every day, and she now lives by the following mantras:

> *I am a great daughter.*
> *I am an amazing wife and mother.*
> *I am a strong woman.*
> *I am ME.*

LIFE IS A BLESSING

Cindy has found herself – she is back! The woman who once wanted to die now sees life as the most beautiful experience ever. She feels that being a mother has been the greatest gift, as it has allowed her to grow and to use her life in a positive way. She says, 'Motherhood isn't easy, but it is worth it. I am not perfect, but I continue to be a better person than I was yesterday'. Cindy's now-21-year-old son still lives back east and considers her as his birth mother, not his everyday mother. One day she hopes to see him face-to-face and to explain everything to him. How amazing would that be? That's a story I'd love to write about soon!

At the time of this book's publication, Cindy has been sober for 10 years and 11 months, and counting. How FANTASTIC. Meeting Liza, her best friend, has helped Cindy get through a lot. They haven't yet had the opportunity to meet in person, but one day it will happen. Liza and Cindy met through a direct sales company – the company matched them up as business partners, and they very quickly became friends (as often happens in direct sales partnerships). They became very close because they supported each other personally and professionally when they experienced difficulties. Liza lives in Florida and is saving to fly out to meet Cindy. They hope this happens soon. Oh, how I'd love to help you with this, Cindy!

Cindy's heart is filled with gratitude and she appreciates everyone who has supported her. She says, 'Many thanks to everyone who helped me get my life back. Thank you so much to my life coach Jennifer, for helping me to realise my worth'. Cindy also has a heartfelt message for you: 'Should you be in this place or one similar to mine, know that there is hope for you, and for anyone who may be living in darkness. Don't give up – and if you have a child going through an addiction, never give up hope and NEVER stop loving them. WE DO RECOVER'.

A final note...

If you resonate with any part of Cindy's story but haven't had the courage to seek the help and support you need, then – I beg you – please do so! I'm so glad I took the time to chat with Cindy and follow the compelling pull in my heart to get to know this woman, despite being caught up in my 50th birthday celebrations aboard the cruise ship.

You see, part of my life purpose was in the connection I'd made with Cindy, and I didn't even know it! Although I started following her life on Facebook, I found absolutely no evidence of the story you've just read. I had no idea about the trials she had faced in the past. By the way, it is a good thing that we sometimes don't know exactly what we are stepping into when we feel an intuitive pull to connect with someone. Sometimes we need to follow our heart and reach out to another human being. For me, it was reaching out across the Pacific. Part of my life purpose was to help Cindy, and when you feel called to connect with someone it's likely that they are part of *your* life purpose. You just need to take a risk and follow your heart.

Now, I don't suggest that you take risks of the nature described in Cindy's story. Cindy was a broken woman who was lost and hurt and full of pain. She allowed herself to become a victim of circumstance who spiralled out of control at every turn. Yet, in her words, 'We do recover'. Know that no matter how dark your world may be right now, you can recover – and there is hope.

So, if you are in a dark place, you might be asking where on earth you could start. I recommend that you follow these steps (in any order):

1. Acknowledge that you need help
2. Start taking responsibility for your choices
3. Stop blaming others
4. Forgive yourself – let go of the past
5. Be kind to yourself and others
6. Find things to be thankful for
7. Rebuild your confidence
8. Remove toxic people and self-sabotaging patterns
9. Change your perception
10. Create your life vision

Also, most countries have amazing support services you can call on (if your country is not listed here, please do an online search):

DOMESTIC VIOLENCE

Australia   1800RESPECT – 1800 737 732 (1800RESPECT.org)

UK   Refuge – 0808 2000 247 (refuge.org.uk)

USA   National Domestic Violence Hotline – 1-800-799-7233 (thehotline.org)

SEXUAL ASSAULT

Australia   1800RESPECT – 1800 737 732 (1800RESPECT.org)

UK   Rape Crisis England & Wales – 0808 802 9999 (rapecrisis.org.uk)

Rape Crisis Scotland – 08088 01 03 02 (rapecrisisscotland.org.uk)

The Rowan (Ireland) – 0800 389 4424 (therowan.net)

USA   RAINN – 800-656-HOPE (rainn.org)

SUBSTANCE ABUSE

Australia Alcohol & Drug Foundation – 1300 85 85 84 (adf.org.au/help-support)

UK Recovery.org – 0203 553 0324 (recovery.org.uk)

USA Substance Abuse & Mental Health Services Administration – 1-800-662-HELP (samhsa.gov)

Remember, help is always available, and you should never give up hope. Cindy's life was a continual cycle of pain until she realised she'd had enough and that she was tired of running away from herself. Like Cindy, you are worthy of more – remember that! You can recover from the stings of life, no matter how dark life may have been so far. Cindy now has a vision and a plan for her future. Without a vision, people continually repeat the same patterns. If you feel you are merely surviving, what will you do? Will you choose to reach for LIFE and find a way to thrive? I sure hope so – and I can help you!

Real Women, Real Stories

a special message from...
CINDY

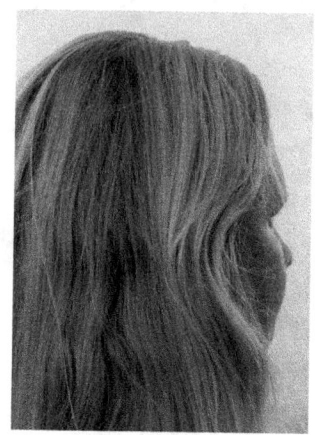

FELICITY S*

* Please note that all names have been changed throughout this story, and that the story features depictions of domestic violence. If you are triggered by this theme I encourage you to access the resources at the story's end.

WAS IT ME?

Before we begin...

I met Felicity in August 2017. I had rocked up to a local writing group, having no real idea about why I chose to attend. But hey – it felt good at the time. I needed to reinvent myself because I had recently been made redundant from my role as a trainer and assessor. I had loved my job, especially because it never really felt like a job. It was everything to me. But back to the story!

Felicity was a regular at the writing sessions and while we didn't forge a deep and meaningful relationship at the time, she stood out to me from the moment I met her. She had wisdom and beautiful qualities to share, and she also shared some life stories that she was still 'living' (which is, essentially, what we are all doing). Felicity loved the sessions and found that the writing activities offered her a release – it's so true that, as women, we often bottle things up and don't feel safe sharing our experiences. After recently working for an organisation that supports women escaping domestic violence, Felicity has now chosen to share her experience here, and I really applaud her courage. Domestic violence is an issue that affects so many women around the world – it could affect you, or other women in your life – and I hope Felicity's story helps you to spot warning signs and reflect on the quality of your relationships.

Felicity's story

'It's hard to express and be open about domestic violence, because I feel it was partly my fault,' Felicity says. However, she now understands that most of the blame lies with her perpetrators.

She had experienced some physical domestic violence in relationships in her 20s and 30s. However, she did not think of those incidents as being 'domestic violence' – she thought that they were merely misunderstandings between a couple. In one of her relationships, she told her new partner that she had been hit in a previous relationship, and he told her that he had not ever, and would not ever, hit a woman. Unfortunately, three years later, he hit her! This was not OK!

At the time, Felicity thought this was her fault. She knew the saying 'it takes two to argue', but she felt she'd caused it because she'd been yelling at him. However, the more she yelled at him after he first hit her, the more he hit her. Again – this was not OK.

Felicity had grown up in a good family and did not experience domestic violence during her childhood. She didn't realise what actions constituted domestic violence. Because of her lack of understanding and because she felt responsible, she did not want to press charges; however, the police were involved, and they pressed charges on her behalf. Looking back, Felicity feels that some of the domestic violence incidents she'd experienced weren't particularly serious. (How often have I heard this? Perhaps you or a friend or loved one are in a similar situation to Felicity and have thought the same thing? Please know that any threatening act is serious.) However, she was soon to experience a whole new level of violence.

AN INNOCENT START

When she was 39 years of age, Felicity started going out with someone new. At the time, she was a single mum of four children (three boys and a younger girl of five years of age, called Lucy) and they lived in a small town where there wasn't much to do. She and her partner, John, had been going out for about six months when they went to a local pub for lunch one Saturday afternoon, and they brought Lucy along. They enjoyed a nice lunch, and John then wanted to sit and have a few drinks with her. At first Felicity said, 'No, I don't want a heavy drink,' as she had just started taking antidepressant medication – John had, in fact, supported her decision to take the medication.

However, despite her initial refusal, she ended up drinking more than one vodka-and-energy-drink combo. A lethal mix! Felicity lost count of how many she had. She felt relaxed and John seemed to be having a nice time.

'Let's go back to my place for a few drinks,' he said.

Felicity was hesitant to go because she was feeling heavily affected by the alcohol, and there wasn't much to do at his home. She didn't want to come to a standstill by going there – she wanted to keep busy. Also, there wasn't much for Lucy to do there. However, lunch was well and truly over, and the sun was starting to set.

So, they ended up piling into a courtesy bus, and drove to his place. When they arrived, they walked into the living room. Felicity needed to pee and quickly went to the toilet. When she came back to the living room John was on the lounge, falling asleep.

'This part of my story is a big blur,' says Felicity.

A SHOCKING NIGHTMARE MADE REAL

Felicity feels that she blacked out and, when she came to, she recalls that she was screaming… and screaming!

Felicity realised she was in John's bedroom, with her body pressed up against the window. His hands were pushing hard against her head – one hand was on her forehead and the other was on her mouth… or was it her throat? All she could do was scream and struggle.

Lucy was by herself in the next room.

While Felicity was screaming and trying to break free from John's grip, she heard the shatter of glass behind her head as he pushed her harder against the bedroom window.

She saw a jagged piece of glass sitting on the window ledge.

Felicity finally broke free and tried to make her way to the bedroom door. While crawling over the bed's mattress, she felt nauseous. Vomit flowed out of her mouth and onto the bed. He yelled at her. There was nothing she could do to stop the vomit, and she made her way off the bed and through the door to find Lucy.

Felicity grabbed her and they quickly headed to the front door. As she went through the door into the dark night, she felt confused and scared and didn't know which way to go.

While Felicity was screaming and trying to break free from John's grip, she heard the shatter of glass behind her head as he pushed her harder against the bedroom window.

She saw people in the street and, feeling ashamed for having screamed so loudly, said, 'I'm sorry,' as she hurried away from the house.

They walked two houses away and sat in the gutter. A lovely woman took Lucy into her home and comforted her. Sitting with her head in her hands, feeling dazed and confused, Felicity looked up to see a smirk on John's face as he was escorted into the back of a police van.

He then glared at her as the van drove away.

When Felicity tells her story now, she feels heavy and confused, and finds it difficult to recall the details of the night – however, she definitely remembers the feeling of overwhelming fear.

She gave up alcohol the day after (although only for a year).

THE AFTERMATH

A few days after the event, Felicity and John met up to talk about what had happened. They met in a park. He told her that she had started it by hitting him to wake him up – she had done this once before. She acknowledged that she had done this on another occasion; however, for this event she didn't remember anything. She wondered whether John was deliberately putting doubts into her head and placing the blame on her. He cried and pleaded with her.

So, she decided not to press charges.

They ended up seeing each other again. He took Felicity, Lucy and one of her sons on a holiday and they went to a theme park. He bought gifts for Felicity and Lucy. She thought things were going well, but it didn't last long.

He broke it off with her and didn't really give a reason.

A few days later, Felicity was feeling upset, angry and hurt. She decided to go to John's house to try to talk things through. (As women, it's so common for us to try to fix things.) However, John was an alcoholic and had been drinking heavily, so he didn't want to discuss anything. Felicity felt so angry and wanted revenge – so, as she was leaving his house, she decided to take his dog home with her. She knew that the one thing that would hurt him would be the loss of his dog, and she also justified her decision by the fact that he didn't treat the dog well.

Felicity was still hurting, and seeking comfort, so she sent a message to her friend, Samantha. However, Samantha messaged back to tell her she was busy having drinks at her parents' house. Felicity didn't want to intrude, so she chose to have an early night, trying to forget about the hurt she was feeling.

The next morning, she decided to take the dog back to John's place. She realised that what she had done was not right. However, when she got to his house the door was wide open, so she went inside. John was asleep on the lounge and his phone was on the ground. The phone rang, and he didn't wake up. So, Felicity looked at the phone. She saw intimate text messages from Samantha, and the last phone call recorded on his phone was also from her. Felicity rang the number, and Samantha answered.

'Hello,' Felicity said.

Samantha hung up the phone.

However, that is another story...

WHO'S RESPONSIBLE?

Looking back, and with the knowledge she has since gained about the nature of domestic violence, Felicity realises that she had been manipulated. After the domestic violence incident, John had most likely cried and tried to buy her affection so that she would not press charges against him. Although (as mentioned) they did reunite briefly after that incident, it wasn't long before he broke off their relationship completely.

Felicity says, 'I still don't understand DV [domestic violence] fully. I am confused about what is a normal relationship and what is a DV relationship. I don't know whether I'm experiencing emotional DV or if I'm overreacting to something that has happened. I don't know if I've been manipulated to believe that I am just a drama queen. I have so many uncertainties'.

At the domestic violence support organisation Felicity worked for, staff always believe a woman's side of the story. However, Felicity still feels responsible for some of the incidents that have happened in her life. She doesn't really know who is at fault. As mentioned, she understands that it takes two people to engage in a situation. She also understands that she has to take responsibility for her actions. However, she wonders whether this 'taking responsibility' approach means she must be the one who ultimately caused a violent situation. Felicity now understands so much more about herself and about domestic violence than when these incidents occurred, and she is willing to learn, to heal, and to value her emotional and physical safety, and to notice and take action if future relationships start to become unhealthy.

Felicity wants to leave you with this quote by Audrey Kitching:

'Forgive yourself for not knowing better at the time. Forgive yourself for giving away your power. Forgive yourself for past behaviours. Forgive yourself for the survival patterns and traits you picked up while enduring trauma. Forgive yourself for being who you needed to be.'

A final note...

I wonder how many women in relationships ask themselves if they are just overreacting or being a drama queen – these were some of the questions Felicity asked of herself.

When it comes to relationships, we can often experience confused feelings if we let ourselves lose our identity, our confidence in who we are and our belief that life will work out for the best. This is certainly something I've experienced, and I long to help other women (especially young women) not fall into this trap.

Once we become emotionally and physically involved with a partner, we can become desensitised to reality. If this happens, we really need a close and trusted friend who is willing to speak truth to us, and to speak that truth in a way in which we will listen. I say this with authority, because there have been many occasions on which I have been blinded by 'love'. I know I was a very stubborn woman (in fact, I still am! ☺). I often didn't listen to my heart, nor did I listen to reality and the advice of others. I was blinded as to what was really happening. I realise now that this was out of a need to be needed, to be loved and to have a man in my life. I was seeking my sense of value in all the wrong things.

Relationships of any sort need to have boundaries, and as women we need to know where we start and end, as well as what we are responsible for and what we are NOT responsible for. As humans in relationships we are going to trigger each other – that's normal; that's life – but how you react to those triggers is what you as an individual are responsible for.

For example: *You get into an argument (or even a simple disagreement) with another person and start yelling at them. You may even have started it. You antagonise the* *other person, and they retaliate. You are not responsible for their actions – they are. You are only responsible for your responses. In no way do you deserve to be abused.*

Domestic violence is a complex area when it comes to laws and charges… I'm not an expert on the subject but I know it's important to be clear about this: violence and abuse of any sort is not OK, whether it's by a man or woman or child. **It's *not* OK.** My father told me something years ago. To this day I remember what he said, very clearly. He said, 'What is abuse? I'll tell you – it's any time anyone ever threatens you, whether it be with fists in your face or with intimidating threats such as bullying or yelling. Those things alone are abuse; it doesn't need to be someone striking you'. The mere threat of danger and intimidation towards you is abuse and constitutes domestic violence.

The sad truth is that many women become repeat victims of domestic violence because they don't realise their worth and often search for that validation in all the wrong places. Many years ago, I helped a younger woman out of a terrible physically and emotionally violent situation – I organised packing boxes, trailers, manpower and a babysitter for her son, and found her a place to live and storage for all her belongings. Within a week she had moved back into the same situation, with all of the promises of a bright future and the hope that things would be different.

Why do you think we, as women, do this? We go back because we believe the perpetrator has somehow miraculously changed; we go back because we don't believe in our value and worth; we go back because we think it's our fault; and we go back because we believe if only *we* were better, they would treat us better. However, this is not the case! We were attacked because of the way the perpetrator feels about themselves, and because we took responsibility for *their* behaviour.

We need to know our worth and value. We need to know who we are. We need to create a clear picture of what we want our lives to look like. We need to define our values and to know that we are valuable. Realising all of this will cause us to say 'NO' to being abused, on any level. In fact, I feel so strongly about this (in case you can't tell!) that I now coach women to create a vision for their life, and to make empowered decisions that truly do change their lives for the better.

You can choose to make a change in your life if you recognise that you are experiencing domestic violence (see later in this section for the signs to look out for). However, if you are feeling powerless to make changes, I suggest following these simple steps:

1. Commit to journaling daily (believe me, it makes all the difference and it's like having your own therapist on call)
2. Acknowledge truthfully the experiences you've had and the effects you feel from them
3. Tell someone you trust about the situation you're in (you can even get in touch with me), or make the phone call to a domestic violence hotline (see later in this section) – asking for help is a crucial step when making a change
4. Commit to finding out who you are and what you love
5. Acknowledge that you deserve to be cared for – there is no wrong way to care for yourself (you need to determine what is right for you)
6. Make exercise and physical activity an enjoyable part of daily life
7. Eat regular healthy meals
8. Look at the blue sky as often as you can – yes, it makes a difference to how you feel!

9. Sleep – you need healthy sleep patterns
10. Read – even if you gave up reading a while ago (although novels are great, for your personal growth I recommend you start reading inspirational books – including the one you're holding in your hands!)

This list is only a starting point. Choosing to grow as a person is one of the most important things you can do for yourself. Every challenge in life – including an experience of domestic violence – can be turned into an opportunity to grow. Never underestimate yourself, your courage, your bravery, your skills and your personality, and use any challenges you face as fuel to change your life.

If you feel as confused as Felicity does about what actions constitute domestic violence, I think it's a good idea to share with you some definitions from www.1800RESPECT.org.au (please do visit the site for more information and for support):

WHAT DOES DOMESTIC AND FAMILY VIOLENCE INVOLVE?

Domestic and family violence can involve behaviour that:

- *Is violent and can, but does not have to be, physical. Violent behaviour can include:*
    - *Sexual violence*
    - *Physical violence*
    - *Psychological or emotional violence*
    - *Financial violence*
    - *Spiritual violence*
    - *Social violence*
    - *Legal violence*
    - *Reproductive violence*
    - *Neglect*
    - *Stalking*

- Causes fear
- Stops you from living as you want
- Forces you to behave in ways you don't want

People who use this kind of violence are sometimes called 'perpetrators of violence'.

WHAT FORMS CAN DOMESTIC AND FAMILY VIOLENCE TAKE?

It is never OK for someone in a relationship to:

- Hit, kick and do other things that hurt your body
- Touch you in ways or places you don't want to be touched
- Force you to have sex or do sexual things
- Say and do things that make you feel scared or unsafe
- Take your money or use money to make your life hard
- Damage walls, parts of your home, or your things
- Tell you they will hurt you, your children, your pets, or people you care about
- Say they will hurt themselves if you try to leave
- Share private photos or videos of you online without your permission
- Stop you from following your religion or cultural practices
- Cut you off from friends or family
- Refuse to provide essential care and support for you if they are your parent, guardian, carer or paid support person
- Make looking after a baby hard by not letting you feed or settle your baby
- Scare you by following you, harassing you or refusing to leave you alone

- *Use the legal system to bully or intimidate you*
- *Stop you from making decisions about whether or not to have a baby, or other reproductive issues*
- *Stop you from having medicine you need or from seeing a doctor*
- *Give you medicine you don't need or more medicine than you need*

These are only some things that domestic and family violence may involve. There are many others. If anyone is making you feel scared, worried or unsafe, it is OK to ask for help.

If you live in Australia and you or someone you know is impacted by sexual assault or domestic violence, call 1800RESPECT on **1800 737 732** (perhaps consider keeping the number on your phone, hidden under a fictional female name) or visit 1800RESPECT.org.au. In an emergency, call **000**.

If you live in the UK or the USA, contact these organisations:

UK Refuge – 0808 2000 247 (refuge.org.uk)

USA National Domestic Violence Hotline – 1-800-799-7233 (thehotline.org)

For other countries, please research details for your local domestic violence service.

By the way, we have let Felicity know that if the re-telling of her story has triggered trauma for her, she is able to access domestic violence trauma counselling through 1800RESPECT. Please know that if you are scared about the effects of sharing your experience with someone else, this service is available to you, too.

Perhaps you've never experienced anything even close to domestic violence and cannot relate personally to Felicity's story. However, after reading her story, you may feel empathy and would like to know how you could help other women who find themselves in this situation. If you'd like to help, reach out to your local community. There are so many women who could use your love and support.

There is hope, and there is a better life, after domestic violence. If you are currently a victim of it, you don't need to remain this way for one second longer. I am sending hugs to you and yours who've had to endure, or are in fact currently enduring, this horrid abuse. Let's make a change!

It's one thing to know, intellectually, that you are a victim of domestic violence, but really feeling and accepting that it is currently your truth is the first step towards recovery.

Real Women, Real Stories

a special message from...

FELICITY

SHARYN REID

COMFORT ZONES ARE FOR SISSIES!

Before we begin...

Fun' and 'vivacious' are words that pop into my mind when I think of this lady. Allow me to introduce you to Sharyn Reid, a woman I've grown to love and admire. Sharyn lives life to the full. Right now she's away with a girlfriend, exploring Tasmania. I love Sharyn's sense of adventure; in fact, we recently made a pact that each year we will do something to push ourselves out of our comfort zones. Last year we joined a couple of other ladies from our Connections group to do a 'Thrillseeking Zipline Adventure' – never had I done anything like that before! Sharyn went first, shaking in her boots as she made the climb across the rugged rocks and terrain to the zipline, and then screaming her way across to the other side. It's interesting that many women say they want to have adventures, but so few do – I wonder why we often play it safe... In this story, Sharyn shares some of her life's adventures with us. May she inspire you to leap into your very own adventures!

Sharyn's story

'OK, here goes,' Sharyn says, breathing in deeply. 'Talk about being outside your comfort zone. Let me tell you my story.'

Sharyn and her husband, David, had lived in New Zealand all their lives, and had spent the last 16 years in Christchurch. Then, about seven years ago, they decided to leave their jobs, sell their house and sell or give away all of their belongings. For years they had dreamt of living in Australia. It all started one Christmas, when they had holidayed on Queensland's Sunshine Coast. Once they were back home, they sat and talked about the great time they'd had, and about how the weather was so lovely and warm. Christchurch is known for its freezing temperatures, and they craved the warmth they'd just experienced. Before they knew it, their house was on the market and had sold within six weeks, and they were busily organising a move to the Sunshine Coast (with a quick trip to China thrown in for good measure).

The idea was to live a minimalist life, so they sold most of their things – except for some special pictures, photos, pots and cutlery. You might be wondering why on earth they would want to keep pots and cutlery. Why, they were brand new! Sharyn just couldn't bear to get rid of them. However, she says, 'I was not sad about selling or giving away most of our stuff – it was actually a liberating feeling. I felt empowered, and free to move on to the next stage'. Family would be what she would really miss. She was leaving behind her son and daughter, and four grandchildren. 'That was really tough,' Sharyn recalls.

Once they closed the door on their old life, they headed over to Australia with three suitcases – one for David, and the other two for Sharyn – and her road bike. It felt surreal to be starting life in a new country, and they were both filled with a mix of emotions. Mostly, Sharyn felt great excitement at the prospect of a new adventure. She wondered what the future held and what new experiences they would encounter. However, there were basic 'life' things to be done at the start of the adventure, including getting an Australian drivers' licence and obtaining a Medicare card (this was a feat in itself). It was such an ordeal to gather the required documents, and this caused their stress levels to rise. Thankfully, it all worked out.

Initially, they rented a very small apartment for six weeks. It was about the size of a one-bedroom motel (wasn't it fortunate that they didn't have many possessions?!), but it did have a pool and a spa. Heaven!

THE AGEISM SHOCK

Their next step was to find work. In New Zealand they had owned a very successful small business that serviced and sold machinery. Sharyn had also moonlighted in the hospitality industry for many years, with roles including barista, cashier, waitress and bartender – and she had even worked in management positions. Although she was 50 years of age when they moved to Australia, Sharyn felt young and didn't expect to have any trouble finding a job. However, for the first time in her life she came across ageism. David faced this same experience, and it wasn't one they had contemplated. She says, 'I wasn't told to my face that I was too old for a position. I guess it was a feeling I got at the interviews'. She would look around at the staff and notice that they all seemed to be quite a bit younger than her. She found this very upsetting, as she'd never really worried about her age. 'It's just a number to me,' she says.

Eventually, though, Sharyn found a bar job at a golf club, and David secured his first job a month after. Sharyn worked at the golf club for just over a year, and it was a fun time. She worked in the bar during the week and then on most weekends she waitressed and helped wedding events to run smoothly (weddings are such happy occasions!). Then she moved to a bowls' club as a bar manager. Sharyn learned how to play bowls while she was there. However, sometimes it all felt a little underwhelming and she often wished 'wine o'clock' would roll around quickly.

THE FRIENDSHIP CHALLENGE

Relocating to a new country and making a home in a new town or city is not always easy. Sharyn found the Sunshine Coast, in particular, to be a tight-knit community, and it was very hard to make friends. She says, 'You have to put yourself out of your comfort zone and make a big effort to meet people as they don't just come to you'. So, she joined a women's gym, a cycling club (because she had her road bike) and various meet-up groups and local clubs. Sharyn craved female friends so that she could do girlie things such as coffee, lunches, shopping and shows, and she really hoped to make friends within these groups and clubs.

However, when she first joined them, Sharyn would often say 'Hi' and try to start conversations but receive only short, one-worded responses – and she felt left out because she didn't know the people or places being discussed in other conversations. She would smile and nod, trying to listen intently and get involved. All the while, she would be feeling dejected and lonely. However, whenever she felt rejection, it only made her work harder to develop friendships. She made the decision to be courageous and keep showing up. Eventually, she managed to contribute more to the conversations. These were much happier times. A friend of Sharyn's once told her, 'If you want to get someone to talk to you, ask them a question about themselves. We all like to talk about ourselves'.

This is such an interesting point... Often, we forget what it's like to be a newcomer. I can tell you that, from hosting our Connections Coffee'n'Chats meet-ups for more than two years and often encountering new women at each gathering, I've noticed that so many women experience these same feelings. It's so important to make room for people. Sharyn has been an amazing host at our meet-ups and has contributed in positive ways to welcoming our new women. Sometimes women don't leave their homes and attend functions or groups for fear of what others will think. They wonder whether they will fit in, whether they are wearing the right clothing, whether they are 'too much' or whether they are enough. A thousand questions roll through their minds. As the host of my group I, too, have had the same questions and fears – from the position of host and as an attendee. We shouldn't judge those we meet. We need to be ready to accept people as they are, and where they are. We don't know what courage it took for them to be there in that moment.

Because she faced the challenge of trying to make new friends so early in her Australian adventure, Sharyn is bolder than ever. She believes that you have to be brave and introduce yourself to someone. 'You never know what great friendships you might make, and it's more fun to share than to hold back and stay quiet. I've grown so much in my confidence by being open to new people and new experiences. This has mostly come about just by *doing* it.' This is such a great reminder: stop talking and start doing.

LESSONS FROM LIFE ON THE ROAD

After two years on the Sunshine Coast, Sharyn and David decided it was time for the next leg of their Aussie adventure. They sold their newly built house and all their belongings and bought a 30ft Mercedes bus that had been converted into a motorhome. Their intention was to work and travel around Australia. Fortunately, not far into their journey, they landed a six-month job in Birdsville, as caretaker tour guides. This involved work at the airport, including booking in passengers, having radio contact with pilots, loading and unloading luggage, and standing on the tarmac directing in the planes. These are things that Sharyn had not, in her wildest dreams, ever thought she would do. She loved the experience. She also worked at Birdsville's information centre. 'That was a great job,' she says, 'as lots of people travel to the outback in the March to November season'.

Sharyn also made the effort to immerse herself in Birdsville's small community, attending many events so that she could meet people and get involved. If you've never been to Birdsville, just know that it is a very isolated town (about 500km from its nearest town) and is very hot and dry… a far cry from the cold of Christchurch. It's a thriving and diverse place, with good ol'-fashioned values. However, Sharyn says, 'Don't stand still or you'll be surrounded by a big black cloud – of flies, that is!'

Three-quarters of the way through their Birdsville contract, David was asked if he would be interested in driving a 30ft product-demonstration show truck around Australia. Sharyn would be able to travel with him. 'Hmm… get paid and be able to stay in hotels and motels. A no-brainer, from my point of view,' Sharyn says. Once their Birdsville stint was up, they headed off to start the next adventure with the truck.

Australia is a beautiful place and Sharyn felt very fortunate to be able to spend almost two years in the truck, taking in all the sights – they travelled huge distances and looped around the country twice. For the first time in her adult life, she was not working. It was a wonderful liberating feeling. She would go out walking or biking for the day, exploring each new location. She felt very fortunate and thankful to have this time. Travelling in the truck was an interesting experience, and there was so much country to see. They would often stop in small towns and sometimes Sharyn would just walk along the main street and window-shop. Sometimes she'd go into a shop to look around and not walk out until half an hour later. Often the shopkeeper would just like to chat, as she had been the only person to walk into their shop all day. Sharyn says, 'I have become used to just starting up a conversation. It's not an easy feat. But it can be rewarding'. Sharyn reminds us again of that great piece of advice given to her by her friend – basically, if you want to chat to someone, the best thing to do is to ask them a question about themselves. Then, you're in! 'It works. You try it!' Sharyn says.

After two years on the road, it was time to park up the truck and move on to the next adventure. Sharyn says, 'It was the end of a perfect time for me'. There had been very little cooking, no cleaning, no making beds... just getting up every morning and hopping on her bike, or walking and exploring. This sounds fantastic!

WHEREVER SHE LAYS HER HAT...

Next stop – Townsville, a coastal city in northern Queensland. Sharyn has found it to be a very friendly place. There are lots of things happening around town and lots of groups with which you can be involved. It's been almost two years since they arrived there, bringing with them a car full to the top with their belongings. They spent three weeks in a motel while they found somewhere to rent. They later bought a house and, yes, new furniture. 'Not many people get to buy three houseloads of new furniture in their lifetime,' Sharyn says, '... and I'm pretty sure I will get to do it again'. She has also found a job as a customer service officer, which she really enjoys, and has joined a few groups and made some wonderful friendships. I was thrilled and surprised when Sharyn rang to invite me to coffee some two years ago. She just wanted to get to know me better! This started a beautiful friendship, with both of us understanding the courage it takes to reach out when you're a newcomer. We also both love Townsville, with its relaxed mix of 'big country town' and 'seaside city'. At the time of writing, Sharyn is preparing to stretch out of her comfort zone for her next adventure – David's job is transferring to Brisbane, so they will be selling their Townsville house and making yet another exciting move.

However, Sharyn says, 'I know these years in Australia sound as though I've had a lovely time. And they certainly have been. But not everything is sugar'n'spice and all things nice'. When it comes to meeting new people, Sharyn has found that it can all feel too hard. She says, 'Your self-esteem can get a bit of a knock when you try to engage with people and you get nothing back. Sometimes, when that happens I just think "bugger it", and I move on to the next person and hope for a friendlier outcome'. Sharyn realises she really has grown her 'friend-making muscles' through her time in Australia, and now she has a beautiful network of friends all over the country. I created my Connections Coffee'n'Chats because I know there are many women who feel isolated when they move to a new town or city. If you're in this situation, draw strength from Sharyn and reach out to others!

FACING THE TUNNEL OF TERROR

Sharyn has always been scared of being in tight spaces. She has been scared of feeling restricted and not being able to get out, and she believes that this might stem from some things that happened in her childhood.

However, as you've seen already from her willingness to take on a life of adventure, it has always been Sharyn's goal to push herself out of her comfort zone. She doesn't want to be held back by her shortcomings. She says, 'It is just about setting yourself up for discomfort in a way that is a little more comfortable'. This means that she is supporting herself as much as she can when she steps out of her comfort zone. For example, to help her with her fear of tight spaces when she flies on a plane, she asks for an aisle seat that is as close as possible to the exits.

Recently, Sharyn and a friend took a trip to Vietnam. 'It was great,' she says. They went to the Củ Chi tunnels. She was so scared at the thought of going through the first tunnel that she made the decision not to do it. The tunnels are very, very tight, and Sharyn says, 'Above ground I fought with myself, knowing that I'd come all the way to Vietnam to do this, yet, in my mind, I was wimping out'. She became so annoyed with herself that she was almost crying. So, she made up her mind to do it. The first tunnel was 22m in length, and she was so scared that she decided to take her mind off her fear by counting out each metre in her steps. Although the tunnels have been widened slightly for tourists, you aren't able to stand up while making your way through. Sharyn therefore walked each step while bent over at a 90-degree angle. 'I felt sick with terror,' she says. She remembers that the walls and floors were so cold, dry and smooth, and it was extremely dark. She actually bumped headlong into the bum of the person in front of her because she was concentrating so hard on her step count. However, the counting kept her somewhat calm, even though her heart was racing the entire time.

Sharyn felt immense relief when she came out of the tunnel. She was overwhelmed by the extreme pride she had in herself, knowing that she had pushed through her fear. Sharyn has come to realise that she is a very determined person: 'Once I have an idea, I work hard to achieve my goal. Although, just to be clear, I'm not saying I would do that *particular* experience again!'

'Above ground I fought with myself, knowing that I'd come all the way to Vietnam to do this, yet, in my mind, I was wimping out.'

THE VALUE OF RELATIONSHIP

We all have our own mantras (positive or negative – you get to choose!) and values in life. For Sharyn, honesty and loyalty are hugely important values. She believes you should treat people the way you want to be treated. On the other hand, don't let the negative speech or actions of others make you feel bad about yourself; if they treat you that way, they are not your friend. And importantly, always listen to the little person in your head (your intuition) – your first thought about a situation is usually right.

Sharyn has also realised that friends are so important in her life. She may not see them for a week, a month, a year – hell, even five years – but when she catches up with them, it is as easy as though it was yesterday. This makes her really happy. Sharyn has one friend she doesn't see often, but when she calls they are laughing within a minute of saying 'Hi!' Sharyn really appreciates that friendship, and she is thankful for all the people who have come and gone from her life. She says, 'These people have given me a lifetime of awesomeness'. She is looking forward to meeting many more amazing people and having adventures with them. Although so much is happening in Sharyn's life, she always has time for friends and family. How about you? Have you invested time and love into developing real connections with your friends and family? I truly believe that our future is determined by the company we keep – we are the sum total of the five people with whom we spend most of our time.

It's important to note that Sharyn believes our human needs cannot be met by just one friend, or one partner. We need a circle of friends. She says, 'I have my sporting friends, my movie friends, my dinner friends, my travel friends... and they are all equally important to me and all contribute to my life in a different way. Please don't put all your eggs in one basket and suck the life out of just one person. It's not how we are meant to live'.

TAPPING INTO SOMETHING DEEPER...

There's something you need to know about Sharyn: she loves music. Sometimes she likes to play calming music, and at other times she wants the bass booming out – and the louder, the better. (Her tastes run the gamut from *Love on the Rocks* by Poison to *Hallelujah* by Stan Walker!) For Sharyn, music evokes powerful emotions, and it often takes her back to a certain time and place. You will regularly find her singing in her car at the top of her voice, with music on full volume, not caring that anyone might be watching. I love doing this at the end of my rideshare shifts in the GlamMobile – I crank up the music, flick on the cruise control and enjoy the uninterrupted ride home!

Every now and then, Sharyn will see or hear something that inspires her to write a poem. Interestingly, she's noticed that her poem-writing is usually triggered by something sad and deep. She's written the following sombre poem, and would like to share it with you:

Heart Broken
My heart is broken
I feel empty inside
I feel alone in this sadness
I just can't hide

Sharyn wrote this poem when she saw a picture of a hollow statue. She felt that the statue just screamed of sadness, hollowness and heartbreak – these are feelings that most of us, if not all of us, have experienced at various points in our lives. She wonders whether her strong desire to live outside of her comfort zone and seek a life of adventure and freedom are connected to her wanting to avoid sadness and despair.

Sharyn says, 'My emotions are very strong. It's interesting how different things or people can bring out different feelings in me'.

AGE IS JUST A NUMBER

When she looks back over her life, she realises that she has a fear of getting old, a fear of not taking chances and not having experiences, and a fear of being lonely. (I have found that many women are afraid of these things, no matter their age – none of us are immune.) However, she knows that she has the choice to act, despite her fears. She sometimes bristles with annoyance when she feels people judge her for her age, and she tries not to let it affect her. She reminds herself of the advice she wants to share with you here: 'You are *never* too old to achieve anything you want to. Don't let other people's perceptions stop you from achieving your goals'. Sharyn loves life and wants to have so many more experiences. 'I never want to hear myself say, "I wish I could do that".' Instead, she wants to always say, 'Where? When? How?' and 'YES, I can'.

For example, when Sharyn was asked if she would like to contribute to this book, she thought, 'I don't think so. I'm not good with words in any format and it is so far out of my comfort zone'. She felt she couldn't possibly contribute anything that someone would like to read or be inspired by. However, Sharyn suddenly remembered her own personal mantra: 'You can do this; it's just another adventure, and I love adventures'.

THE HAPPY BALANCE

Even when her life has its low points, Sharyn's glass is always half-full. She really is a positive person: 'I am an optimist – I tend to look on the happier, more-positive side of life, and I endeavour to make the most out of the situations that occur in my life'. She rarely passes up the chance to travel, and she also finds exercise to be very therapeutic, noting that '... a good, long hard walk or an hour in the pool helps to flush out any negativity'. On the other hand, she says, a couple of glasses of good Merlot doesn't hurt, either.

'Let's get out there and explore, have adventures, meet people and make memories,' she says, '... and remember that only you can make yourself happy'. (I'm loving this fantastic advice – we all need this!) After taking that leap of faith – selling nearly everything and leaving Christchurch to start a new life in Australia, at age 50 – Sharyn is definitely making the best of her life. 'What matters to me,' she says, 'are people and experiences'.

A final note...

Sharyn, thank you so much for stepping out of your comfort zone and sharing parts of your life story with our readers. I've always found your approach to life to be inspiring, regardless of all of the curveballs that have been thrown at you. It takes courage to leave a comfortable place and start again. As women, we often settle for the status quo. We avoid pushing past fears that limit us and confine us to the four walls of our homes.

Stepping out of our comfort zones starts in the mind – once we overcome those limiting beliefs, we can do anything. I often say, 'Let's do it afraid'. This means that you shouldn't wait for the feelings of fear to leave (you could be waiting a while!). Instead, *use* the fear to 'do it anyway'. You see, our brains are programmed to keep us safe, so fearful feelings come to the surface for a reason. Our subconscious mind wants us to stay in the safe zone and not ever experience new things. Fear has the same emotional feeling as excitement, but our brains tell us to stay in that safe zone – therefore, we need to rewire our neural pathways and push past the fear. It's then that we get to experience and enjoy new things.

I know that there are women who won't leave their houses and come to our Connections Coffee'n'Chats meet-ups because they are letting their fears hold them back. However, what real danger is there outside your four walls? A change in perspective will make all the difference. As Sharyn says, if people don't embrace you in a conversation, simply move on to the next person. She advises not letting someone else's speech or actions make you feel bad about yourself.

I also loved this other piece of amazing advice from Sharyn: 'Only you can make yourself happy'. You see, your happiness comes from within – choose to embrace who you are, allow yourself to be authentic, and believe in yourself! We are all created to be unique, and the majority of us also desire an adventure and friends with whom to share it. Remember that good-quality relationships are known to make us happy and are definitely worth pursuing and cultivating. We are not meant to be an island – we were created for relationships and friendship. The problem is, we allow our fears and insecurities to keep us locked away.

Sharyn could have given up on the idea of making new friends, but she chose to keep starting new conversations with different people. This would not have been easy, but she was tenacious. When we are not immediately embraced and accepted, most of us give up and think that there is something wrong with us. However, the reality is that we are not everyone's cup of tea. We just need to find the connections that are meant for us. This takes time and courage. It also takes a willingness to continually step out of our comfort zones and let down our walls, never giving up – no matter what our brains are trying to tell us.

When it comes to our age, let's not allow a certain number to hinder us from living an amazing life – let's do it afraid, regardless! Every day is an opportunity to embrace a new adventure of some sort, no matter how big (like feeling claustrophobic yet crawling through the Củ Chi tunnels in Vietnam – see the look of elation and relief on Sharyn's face in the photo at the end of this chapter!) or how small (like leaving the house and sharing a smile).

After reading Sharyn's story, I have absolutely no doubt that you're feeling inspired to leave your comfort zone. I know I am – in fact, every time I've read her story throughout the production of this book, I've been reminded of the power and choice we all have. You really can live your best life!

Comfort Zones Are for Sissies!

a special message from...

SHARYN

SANDRA HUBERT

I'LL DO IT MYSELF

Before we begin...

I feel so honoured to share Sandra's story with you. We first met online in the social media world and we kept in contact consistently via Messenger. Little did I know that she only lived just down the road from me. Whatever has happened to the old tradition of popping in to a neighbour's house for coffee, tea or wine?! Anyway, one day Sandra invited me to come to a 'WOW' lunch – WOW stands for 'Women of Worth'. Since meeting her in person and coming to know her, one thing I know for sure is that Sandra certainly is a woman of worth. She is definitely worthy of celebration, for having overcome such shocking adversity – interestingly, I had no idea about Sandra's profoundly life-changing experience until very recently. I know you will find her story compelling – every time I read it, I'm reminded that each and every one of us has what it takes to get through <u>anything</u>!

Sandra's story

She stood there as a four-year-old with hands on her hips, telling everyone, 'I'll do it myself'. Since that time, this has been Sandra's mantra. However, back then, she didn't realise that she would need this strength and determination at the age of 31.

In May 1993 Sandra's 30th birthday was looming, and she was reflecting on her life while planning her birthday party. Sandra had a wonderful husband (Roland) of nine years, two awesome sons, a home, great friends, lots of family and a fabulous job. Her job had the potential to fulfil her career goals as a management accountant. It sounds to me like Sandra had a vision for her life... When she reflected on the fact that she had two children, she thought, 'Don't I want three or maybe even four children?' Sandra and Roland discussed it, and at Christmas they announced to the family the good news that baby number three was on its way.

TRAGEDY STRIKES

At 8½ months into the pregnancy, Sandra was preparing her job for maternity leave and everything was going well. Yes, she had pains and a headache, felt warm and was going to the toilet often, but her weekly doctor visits showed she was healthy. Oh, how wrong they all were. On Wednesday 3 August 1994, Sandra declined a dinner invitation because she had the worst pain at the back of her head. She went to bed, but during the night Roland woke to her having a grand mal seizure, so he immediately rang the ambulance.

Their awesome neighbours jumped the fence to look after their boys (aged seven and nine). They needed two ambulances because Sandra's seizures wouldn't stop and two people had to work on her at once. The obstetrician met the ambulance at their private hospital. He knew straight away that Sandra's symptoms weren't baby related, and he called in a neurologist.

The medical team did heaps of tests – lumbar punctures, an MRI, CAT scans and bloods – and tried many different medications to stop the seizures and bring down her temperature. However, on day two the team decided they didn't have the time to wait for test results. Instead, they arranged to transfer Sandra to Townsville Hospital, which, at the time, didn't have a birth suite at that location – this meant that all of the baby-delivering equipment would need to be brought from the hospital's other location for an emergency caesarean. Within minutes of Sandra arriving at the hospital, their third son was delivered at a healthy 6lb 14oz and Sandra was placed into a coma. She was diagnosed with a severe strain of viral encephalitis and they needed to stop her brain functioning to give it time to heal.

Sandra's scans revealed extensive brain damage to the right temporal lobe. She was given less than a 1% chance of survival. If she did survive, her doctors thought she would be paralysed down her left side and need 24/7 care. The dose Sandra received of antiviral drug acyclovir was tripled because they were doing all they could to save her life. It was up to her now.

Shortly after his birth, Sandra's son was taken to the hospital's maternity location, 20km away – however, the awesome staff would bring her son to visit her every day. This allowed her to start bonding with her little boy, and being able to see him gave her a reason to live. The staff went above and beyond, and she is so grateful for all that they did.

During Sandra's 10 days in a coma Roland rarely left her side. He talked to her, reminding her of all the things they had done together. The staff in intensive care were wonderful, and the neurologist kept Roland informed at all stages. No matter what happened or how much support she needed, Roland told her that he was taking her home. Three weeks later, Sandra slowly walked out of the hospital. The power of the mind and of words is incredible. I wonder if Roland truly knew the effects, at the time, of his constant positive reinforcement?

LIFE WILL NEVER BE THE SAME

After coming out of the coma, Sandra was disoriented, she had no short-term memory and her balance was gone. Basically, the light was on and nobody was home. Sandra had to re-learn everything. Every time she went to the toilet at the hospital, she would ask the staff where it was and would look in every room until she found it. Then she would repeat this process until she found her room again. The staff would just watch her; Sandra was determined to find her way on her own. Sandra now says, 'Do you hear that? "I'll do it myself" was back'.

Their new son had been taken home from hospital before Sandra, and the family at home had the wonderful support of extended family and friends. Family members rotated to stay with them; first came her mum, then her sister, then her grandma. Friends cooked meals so that Roland could concentrate on looking after their two young boys, a newborn and her, plus work. Roland says, 'Any man who says he can look after a newborn and work is telling fibs'. He wanted to do it all – work *and* feed his baby son. 'I'll stay up and do his next feed, I'll get up during the night,' he told Sandra's mum. On day three, her exhausted husband slept through the night, not hearing his little son's cries. But that's OK, as Nana was there to take over. 'What would we do without family?' asks Sandra.

She found day-to-day living hard. She couldn't remember who had just left the room or what they had just spoken about. Sandra is an avid reader but couldn't read because she didn't know what the words meant. So, she started to study the dictionary and her handy thesaurus. However, she still found it hard to read a book because she couldn't remember what she had just read. Sandra couldn't even watch a movie because she had facial recognition problems, meaning that most people looked alike to her, and she would forget what had just happened. Sandra knew instantly anyone from her past but new people were difficult to remember.

Sandra often sat in their lounge room staring at their wedding photo, looking at the man holding her hand. She knew he loved her and that they had had a life together. Sandra had to find all her memories and put everything back together. She was like the proverbial favourite china bowl that had been dropped and was now in a million pieces. She had loved the bowl that was her old life, so she had to pick up each piece one at a time, and glue it back together. 'Glue me back together. How do I do this?' Sandra asked herself.

Sandra was determined to work on her short-term memory, so she started playing the card game 'Patience'. She played all day. Sandra first had to remember red and black and numbers, and then she worked on the four suites until she could play a game properly. She also had balance issues – the floor looked like an ocean to her, and as she walked she would stumble and almost fall over. Roland would catch her and smile. He'd say, 'See? I've still got it. You looked at me and the earth moved'. They'd both smile and hug, which made a world of difference. Roland was her rock. He often held her hand and hugged her. Sandra says, 'Roland made me feel like I was "me" again. In his arms I didn't have to remember who I was, what was happening or what to do. I could just be me and feel real again'.

There she was in her own home of six years, but she kept getting lost. She would walk up the hallway and turn right and wonder where her bedroom was. She was automatically taking the route she would have taken to her childhood bedroom, so it gave her hope that, perhaps, her memories

She was like the proverbial favourite china bowl that had been dropped and was now in a million pieces.

were still in her brain and she just had to bring them forth. Sandra had to re-learn all previously learned behaviour (such as how to function on an everyday level) and to manage and identify emotions. For example, if one of her children came to her with a cut finger, she had to work out how to feel and how to determine the logical steps to be taken. Frustration and fear were emotions she came to know all too well, but she also acted with determination. And an amazing sense of resilience, I'd say!

BABY STEPS

Sandra sat at the table with pen and paper, intending to write down how she felt. She had done a lot of diary-writing and planning in her past life, and instinct told her that writing would help bring back the old Sandra. The pen shook in her hand. She could see the words in her head, and she stared at her hand, willing it to move. The page was blank. The pen began quivering in her hand as she concentrated on it with all her might, determined to make it move. But... nothing. She breathed deeply and commanded her hand to stop shaking. Sandra pushed the pen onto the writing pad – she looked intently at it, yet could not work out how to move her hand to write.

In frustration, she used her other hand to push the pen, and then pushed her chair back and looked down in delight at the black pen mark on the paper. 'See, it does work,' Sandra thought. So, she once again placed the pen on the paper. This time she moved her shoulder back and forth. This made more pen marks on the page. Sandra smiled. (Wow, I'm smiling, too – and with tears. Can you just imagine this feeling?) Then she moved her elbow, and then her wrist, which triggered a memory and helped her remember how to write. The letters were large and oddly shaped, but it was a start.

In life after her coma, it was as though Sandra was a wonderful actress playing the part of a lady who was married with three children. She had high expectations of herself and she didn't want to fail; however, she often felt like an alien who had come to earth and taken over a lady's body to learn about humans. Sandra knew the part but had to learn how to *feel* the part and not just act it.

Sandra also had to rebuild a relationship with their two older children. It was very hard for them to cope with a mummy who was so unwell. She looked the same as before, but her mannerisms and even her voice were different. Realising that her boys were affected by this broke Sandra's heart, as she loved them and didn't want them to suffer. She loved being a mother and it was the only thing she'd ever really wanted to be. After a few months she started to feel better about herself, so she put on a nice dress and applied her perfume (which she hadn't done since before the coma). All of a sudden, she heard squeals, and her children came running down the hall. Sandra turned around as they jumped up on her bed, their faces lit up. They said, 'You smell like Mummy!' Her eyes welled with tears as she hugged them. In that moment she felt complete. Something of her was real to her boys. She felt like the happiest mum in the world. She always wears perfume now, and her husband says he loves the smell as he knows she's there.

KNOWLEDGE IS POWER

Sandra knew that information cures fear, so off she went to the library to find out all she could about viral encephalitis. She needed to know how the brain worked so that she could stick hers back together and get it working again. She also went out to the psychology unit at James Cook University and had psychometric testing done so that, on paper, she could see how her brain functioned. This helped Sandra immensely in her understanding of the 'why'. She experienced a high level of function in some areas but was average or below average in other areas. This made her feel conflicted because she knew she should be better. Sandra says, 'Average wasn't good enough'.

REMEMBER WHEN?

Sandra was very lucky that her brain injury affected her right temporal lobe because she is left-brain strong – this is reflected in her job as an accountant. She is good with numbers and patterns; she is logical and analytical. After the coma, Sandra converted everything she could to numbers. For example, when she walked the boys to school, she knew they had to take 16 steps and turn right, then take 124 steps and turn left, and then take 47 steps and cross the road to find the school crossing. She reversed this to get home and she was always so happy to see her neighbour's fence, as she knew then that she hadn't become lost. Sandra listened to what she was walking on to help her retrace her steps – grass, gravel and bitumen all have different sounds and she used this to help determine where she was.

Luckily for Sandra, she was still good friends with her teenage friends – those friendships go back decades. They helped put the pieces back together because they would talk all night about the 'Remember when?'s. One dear friend, Craig, who is like family to Sandra, spoke with her for eight hours on the phone. He reminisced about the past, covering all the places they'd been, who did what, and helping her remember. These memories were invaluable. She was then able to remember times when she had been healthy, and it helped her brain remember what it was like before it had been damaged.

Sandra had practically lost her sense of smell, but her hearing was now more acute. Her sense of smell is still complicated – over the past 25 years she has only once smelt rain for one second, and twice smelt coffee for one second. Stick a pooey nappy or chook poo under her nose and she has no clue. Sometimes she can sense a smell in the air but she can't actually smell it. Sandra says, 'I can smell the earthy smell of a potato but I can't smell a ripe mango'.

When it came to her hearing, she was diagnosed with hyperacusis, which means her hearing was too perfect. When her children breathed near her it sounded like a trumpet. She could hear cars coming from miles away and could even hear the neighbour across the road chatting in her kitchen. She heard a friend, who was in a car behind her car, speak to her passenger. The noise nearly drove her mad, as she couldn't concentrate. If people whispered instead of talking out loud, it didn't help because it pushed out more air and made more sounds. However, there was something fun about this condition – it gave her the ability to know when a phone was going to ring. It was a great party trick. Sandra would stand up, walk to a phone, place her hand over it... and it would ring. She did this all the time and the only explanation they could find is that there must be a noise that happens just before the phone rings, and she sensed that.

AGAINST ALL ODDS

Sandra just wanted to be back to her old self, but she struggled with everything. She started experiencing anxiety and agoraphobia. Sandra and Roland realised later that this was because every time they left the house it was to go to a doctor or specialist – it was at those places that Sandra had a needle stuck into her or the doctor talked about her as if she wasn't there. So, of course, she felt that she didn't want to go anywhere, and that she wasn't in control of her own life. She needed a place of peace, a safety zone. She found it in music. Her favourite singer is Phil Collins, and she may have forgotten so much but one thing she could never forget is his music. It reached to the depths of her being and awoke her. On any given day Sandra may not have been able to remember something that had just happened, but she could sing all of Phil's songs. Playing his music relaxed her and helped her anxiety; it also helped her hyperacusis.

Sandra would place an earplug from her iPod in her left ear and have music playing softly. At that volume it distracted her hearing and allowed her to feel almost normal. It calmed her and helped her to remember. Phil Collins' music helped Sandra more than anything else because it made her remember when she was 17 and healthy; the music, along with Craig's reminiscing, helped to rebuild her brain. Also, Roland says, 'The music was good for our marriage'. Why do you think this would be? Well, when he came home and could hear Phil Collins playing, and Sandra was singing and dancing around the house, it meant that she was in a good mood and had had a good day and he could come in and chat with her. If Phil was playing and she was sitting and staring into space, her day had not been good – and she was trying to do something to drag herself out of it. In that case, Roland would hug Sandra and give her time.

It was also Phil Collins who helped Sandra to be able to watch movies. 'How is that?', you ask? Well, she found it too difficult to watch movies – she had to remember what had happened earlier in a movie, keep up with the actors and concentrate on all of the things that were happening. However, when watching Phil Collins concerts on TV, she focused on Phil and was totally wrapped up in the music, the back-up singers and the members of the band. Sandra found that this helped her to enjoy the entire picture and be at one with everything. She then started watching cowboy movies because in those it's easy to work out who are the goodies and who are the baddies – also, the themes are simple.

Phil Collins also helped with her anxiety and agoraphobia. One day she watched one of Phil's concerts and realised that he was only one person and he wasn't scared to walk out on stage with thousands of people watching. *He* wasn't scared, so why was she too scared to walk out her front door? There wasn't even anyone on the other side of the door to see her – why was she so afraid? Sandra made the decision to stand up, walk to her front door (which had been a barrier for weeks), open the door, take a deep breath and step through. It was probably the same feeling a first-time bungy-jumper would have, but for Sandra it was merely putting one foot in front of the other. You know what? Nothing happened. Sandra recalls that she didn't fall to the bottom of the earth; no monster ate her, and she didn't die. She stood on her front veranda and knew that she had made her first step towards recovery.

After Sandra had spent two years on brain-healing medication, her neurologist told her it would now be safe for her to drive. Sandra is very logical, so she studied the street directory and her address book – this meant she knew where to drive. She hopped into the same manual car she had driven before she suffered her brain injury, started the engine, put Phil Collins' *Face Value* album into the tape deck and cranked up the volume. Doing this made her feel the way she did at 17 years of age, so she simply reversed out of the driveway and drove off. If she became disoriented, she would say, 'I haven't turned so therefore I am still on Ross River Road'. It took her a while to adjust to different speeds and different types of roads, but her driving skills (taught by her dad) were still there. Whenever she saw a landmark she recognised, she would smile. 'See? I wasn't lost!' she recalls.

RE-TRAINING HER BRAIN

Sandra needed communication skills because she didn't know what to say or how to say it – this applied whether she was at home or out and about in social situations. So she joined committees and did a speech-craft course. These helped to rebuild her skills, in a structured social environment. She found it more difficult to talk with friends because there was a lack of structure – the topic of conversation changed quickly and it took longer for her to think of something to say, how to say it and what tone to use. By then, the topic had changed. Sandra read up on conversation-starting phrases and also used the work of Allan Pease to decipher body language. She also learned to give herself time to answer questions. When asked a question she would go blank, at first. She felt embarrassed that she couldn't straight away recall something simple, such as how her day was going. She felt there was a flashing sign across her forehead saying, 'She has a brain injury'. However, we all have those moments, so it's OK to say, 'My day, hmmm, where do I start?' When Sandra said this, it gave her brain enough time to put together an answer. Even today she takes a moment to gather her thoughts before answering.

She also made sure she had structure in her life so that she coped with everyday activities such as doing the washing – if the washing machine was covered, it meant all of the washing had been done; if the washing basket was out, then there was washing on the line. She had many prompts like this around the house and office. Sandra wrote lists, and she converted everything to numbers to help her remember. For example, she knew she needed to carry three items, or she'd need to buy five things, or she had four things to do when she got home.

ONCE A DOER, ALWAYS A DOER

Sandra's not a person to sit still, so when she received a flyer requesting someone to help a mum who had a daughter with disability, she put up her hand. Roland would drop her off and pick her up, allowing her to spend a morning or an afternoon helping them out. Incredibly, this was only one year after coming home from hospital! Having lived with a disability, Sandra could offer support with huge amounts of empathy and understanding, and she wanted to give back. To help pay for this young girl's operations and special needs, Sandra, Roland, the girl's mum and a couple of other ladies started a trust fund and began raising money.

Sandra enjoyed working on committees because doing so helped her use her business skills – so she kept joining them. She enjoyed the roles of president, secretary and treasurer for the past students of The Cathedral School of St Anne & St James, and for Wee Care (now known as Althea Projects) and Soroptimist International. These are amazing achievements for anyone, let alone someone who has experienced this level of brain injury. She also joined her local chamber of commerce, and in her first year at the chamber started the Thuringowa Business Awards – Sandra ran the awards each year, involving the community, businesses and media (TV and newspapers). Sandra received a letter from the manager of Townsville's television station saying that her awards night was one of the best organised events he had attended, and he'd attended many events. She was also asked by the Australian Institute of Management to join its executive committee and take on a role with its management awards. The lady who had had an extensive brain injury and had become lost in her own house was being asked by her peers to work alongside them.

'Rebuilding yourself is complicated and a lot of hard work,' says Sandra. She wanted to get back her career so that she could achieve something tangible. She wanted to stand in front of her peers and feel that she was just as good as them and that she wasn't a failure. Sandra *didn't* want pity; she wanted respect. So, after she had been doing committee work for 11 years, and working with her husband in his business, she went out into the world to test herself – and yes, she did test herself.

As a first step back into the world of paid work, Sandra applied for the role of management accountant with a large family organisation. The company's tax agent was on the panel of interviewers, so with this extra pressure she knew she'd have to impress them. The company had 11 different businesses under its umbrella, including farming, retail, wholesale and transportation, in seven different locations. She got the job, and was in her element. She could see that budgets and forecasts needed to be created for the organisation's many different types of farming businesses, but she was told this couldn't be done. However… she did it! Every day at work was a challenge, and she really enjoyed it.

COMING SO FAR…

In 2008, 14 years after viral encephalitis threatened to destroy Sandra's life, she stood on stage with two other ladies. They were the top three finalists for the Townsville Business Women's Network's 'Corporate Business Woman of the Year' award. Only four people in the room of hundreds knew that she'd had a brain injury, so when her name wasn't called as the winner, Sandra says, 'I was already a winner'. There is one special memory Sandra has that shows how far she's come – when she walked into her neurologist's office 10 years after they'd first met, he stopped and looked up at her with his hands open. He shook his head in disbelief and said, 'I still can't believe you are here. You have done so well'.

LIFE NOW

Sandra believes it's something of a miracle that her life is the way it is today. However, from the outside, people can't see what she needs to do to counter the effects of her brain injury – including being systematic about everyday activities and pausing before answering questions. Earlier in her recovery, it was difficult for her to concentrate, because in order to process and store information she needed quiet and few distractions. To be able to concentrate these days she still requires the volume around her to be quiet, and for her to make slow movements or no movements at all. Often, she will still need information to be organised in a sequential way.

Sandra is still unable to smell things, yet she can sense smells by her body's reaction. She can't store recipes in her head (an ability so many of us probably take for granted) so now she cooks by using recipes that have numbered steps – this helps her remember where she is up to. Sandra also struggles with facial recognition, although this only applies to people she didn't know before her brain injury – she always recognises people from before that time. She's learned to ask questions to help remember someone's name if she sees them outside their normal environment (for example, if one of the mums from school says 'Hello' to Sandra at the shops). The hardest things for her to do is give herself that extra second to respond; to not be so hard on herself when she forgets something; and to know it's OK to ask for help. Some days it all becomes too much, but Sandra tells herself that she hasn't come this far to give up now.

For every wall Sandra came to along her recovery journey, she found a way over it or around it. She says, 'I'm not perfect, but I stand tall and look the world in the eye. I stand with my hands on my hips and say, "I'll do it my way" and smile'.

A final note...

GO Sandra! What an inspiring story!

What does Sandra's story evoke within you? She has shown us how she painstakingly, step by step, reclaimed and reinvented her life. I know some people may not agree that you can reinvent yourself and re-learn major life skills such as walking, self-care and writing – but Sandra is living proof that it is possible. Imagine having to get to know your husband and children all over again? If a human has the power to do all of this then *you* can reinvent yourself in any way. Science proves that we can rewire our brains. Please don't try to tell me that your brain can't do this.

If Sandra's story isn't one of reinvention, I don't know what is. The majority of us do not have to re-learn the basics of everyday life. When life has knocked us for six (or 12, as in Sandra's case), it's important to create a new version of ourselves in our minds – we need to take on a new, empowered identity. Oftentimes the biggest obstacles we have are the ones we create in our minds. Our imagination can be used for creating things and for negating things – for rearming and for disarming. It's your choice.

Do you remember that Sandra used a beautiful analogy in her story, an analogy regarding a favourite china bowl? A bowl (her life) that was dropped and was now in a million pieces? She loved that bowl, and so she had to pick up each piece, one at a time, and glue the bowl back together. My question to you is this: do you LOVE YOURSELF enough to truly put yourself back together if you've experienced hardship? Perhaps your experience is not the same as Sandra's, but there's one thing I know for sure – the only way you can really glue yourself back together is to love yourself. If you find that idea hard, start by just accepting yourself!

I meet so many people who say that they have no imagination and no creativity (I'm guilty of saying this of myself, too) – however, we ALL clearly do. We need to reconnect with who we are and allow ourselves to use our imagination positively. In your mind, imagine the life you want – this is your vision. Roland's vision was of his wife being well and whole again. He created this picture with his thoughts and words. He had faith and a belief that she would recover.

Sandra had a vision of being able to function normally once again, and she applied her stubborn determination to see her vision fulfilled. She demonstrated the power of the mind, even though it didn't function the way it once had done. She chose to re-learn the skills she needed and to reinvent her life. If Sandra can do this, you absolutely can, too. She invites you to do as she has done: 'Put your hands on your hips, stand tall and do it your way!' And don't forget to smile!

I'll Do It Myself

a special message from...

SANDRA

LISA ROLLINS

GRIEF-STRUCK

Before we begin...

Grief is something that will visit every person in their life – sadly, it will come to some people much more often than for others. I met Lisa through social media and got to know her at our local Connections Coffee'n'Chats meet-ups. My heart just opened up with love for her the moment I met her. Sometimes there's a beautiful connection between women, isn't there? That instant connection can be deeper than the mind can even imagine – it's a knowing, and a sensing that you share a common experience. All of this is felt even though no words have yet been uttered and therefore no stories have yet been exchanged. This is how it was for me when I met Lisa. When I invited her to share a story for this book, I didn't even know what her story would be or what our common links were. I just knew that I had to ask her... and so here we are. Allow this woman's story to wash over you. Allow it to take you on a journey that reveals how to recover from any type of grief that may have knocked at your door. This highly moving story may well provoke tears, so please be prepared...

Lisa's story

The year 1985 started in a happy, normal way. Lisa was a full-time stay-at-home mum, living in Hobart in southeastern Tasmania. Hobart features beautiful bushland, beaches and views of the amazing Wellington Range. Lisa loved looking out into the distance at the ice-covered peaks. She was married to Peter, and together they shared a beautiful little boy called Matthew John Hayes.

Matthew had been born on 12 November 1983, weighing 7lb 4oz. He was perfect in every way and Lisa and Peter were over the moon at his arrival. Matthew was their first child, and they were first-time parents who felt a combination of all of those first-time-parent emotions – excitement, fear, overwhelm and happiness. They brought Matthew home after seven days in hospital, and he was an unsettled baby to start with. He suffered from colic and his days and nights were very mixed up; he would sleep all day yet be awake all night. Needless to say, Lisa and Peter were exhausted after three months, so they asked for some help to settle him and finally started to enjoy being parents.

Matthew grew into a gorgeous little toddler. He was playful and funny, and he loved learning words. Lisa recalls, 'He started to recognise things and he could say "Mum", "Dad" and "Nan"'. Lisa took delight each and every day when he learnt something new.

However, something unthinkable was about to happen. Lisa says, 'As I recall this, the memories of that fateful night crash around me, bringing waves of endless pain'. Even now, in telling her story so many years later, the pain is just as jagged and sharp, and her tears flow. 'The effect that this experience had on me and on those around me and close to me has never been forgotten. We have all grieved differently.

We have all hurt. We have all felt the pain. But, most of all, we loved and adored this beautiful little boy who came into our lives for such a short time.'

THE NIGHTMARE BEGINS

On 1 August 1985, Lisa picked up Matthew from daycare at 5.30pm. He looked really tired; in fact, they had both had a big day. Lisa and Peter fed him and bathed him, as was their routine most nights. Matthew was a good baby when he finally settled.

At 10.30pm, Lisa went to bed. Peter stayed up to watch the cricket. At around 3am he came into their bedroom and woke her up, saying, 'Lisa, there's something wrong with Matthew'. Lisa went into baby Matthew's room and could hear the rattle in his breathing. She picked him up out of bed. He was very lethargic and not moving much at all. Lisa told Peter to call the ambulance, but while Peter was on the phone to the ambulance and Lisa was sitting in a chair holding her little boy in her arms, he stopped breathing! Oh my goodness, can you imagine this? Can you imagine being in Lisa's shoes? Or perhaps you have also been in this situation?

Lisa laid Matthew down on the floor and noted that he had no heartbeat and no breath – so she started mouth-to-mouth and CPR. However, nothing seemed to work. Peter picked up Matthew in his arms and carried him up and down the hallway, patting him on the back and saying, 'Daddy's here, Daddy's here'. Lisa looked at Peter and knew in her heart that Matthew had died. Lisa's life had just shattered into a million pieces.

When the ambulance arrived, Peter took Matthew out to the paramedics. Lisa remembers being in the lounge thinking, 'Why is this happening?' She walked out of the front door and down the path towards the ambulance. A paramedic came to meet her and said, 'I'm sorry, but your son is dead'. All Lisa remembers is collapsing to her knees and screaming, 'No!' She could not believe what she was hearing. Her beautiful little boy, the little boy she had carried and given birth to had... what? Just passed away in her arms? Lisa's sister, who was staying with Lisa and Peter at this time, had woken when she heard Lisa screaming. Lisa didn't know what to do next, so she rang her parents, who lived about 45 minutes' drive away. Her dad answered the phone and she told him that Matthew had died. Lisa says, 'My dad kept saying to me, "Lisa, don't say that"'. Again she repeated it, 'Matthew has died'. Her dad kept saying, 'Don't say that, don't say that'. Lisa's mum got on the phone and Lisa repeated to her what she had told her dad. How terrifying and surreal for Lisa, Peter and the family.

In a state of complete shock, Lisa's mum and dad got in their car and drove to her straight away. Lisa went out to the ambulance and said, 'Please do not take Matthew until my parents arrive'. They told her that if a call came through, they had to take Matthew. Her parents arrived and were given a short time with Matthew before they took him away. Her sister kept saying, 'If only I had woken up earlier, if only I had heard him earlier... IF ONLY'. Lisa's parents had driven up from Murdunna on the smell of an oily rag, with less than a quarter of a tank of fuel for the 90km journey. To this day, Lisa says, 'It was a miracle that they arrived'.

A STATE OF SHOCK

Lisa doesn't know how long it was until the police arrived. She kept thinking to herself, 'What did I do wrong? How did this happen? Am I going to go to jail? Why are the police here?' All of these questions went around and around in her head. The police questioned both Peter and Lisa. She felt as though she was guilty of something but was unsure of what had gone wrong. Lisa's mother stayed with them as they went through the motions of identifying their son and planning the funeral arrangements. They chose a white coffin for Matthew, with a blue ribbon on it.

Lisa doesn't remember sleeping or eating. She was just so overcome with grief. Millions of things were running through her mind. Although they were united in their grief, Peter and Lisa both grieved differently. Lisa found it hard to go into baby Matthew's room. Sleep became non-existent because the nightmares would start EVERY TIME she closed her eyes… and this continued for many years.

Lisa would pick up Matthew's clothes and hold them close to her, hoping it would make her feel close to him. She would also inhale the smell of Matthew that was on his clothes. She had to pick out clothes that he was to be buried in. She wanted a little piece of everyone close to him to go with him, so he was buried in the jumper that Lisa's mother had knitted, the overalls that his godmother had given him and the shoes that they bought him, and she also added his bottle to comfort him, his dummy to sleep with, a little blue teddy and some photos of his mummy, daddy, grandparents, aunties and uncles.

THE PAIN OF SAYING GOODBYE

The funeral was one of the hardest things that Lisa had ever had to attend. Unbelievably, she had attended her grandfather's funeral less than a month before. Close friends had asked to view Matthew before they closed the coffin, but Lisa vetoed the idea. She wanted them to remember a smiling, happy little boy. Lisa remembers that she and Peter were standing by his coffin before they closed it, and Lisa reached out and held Matthew's hand. She doesn't know how long she stood there but as she held his hand she could feel it getting warm. She looked at Peter and said, 'I think they've made a mistake. Feel him – he is getting warm'. Peter started to cry, as did Lisa. She was grasping at straws because she so desperately wanted to believe that he hadn't died… Lisa could not imagine her life without him.

Matthew had touched the hearts of so many people, and they came to pay their respects to this gorgeous little boy. Lisa really doesn't remember much about the funeral service itself, but she does recall the priest reciting a paragraph from the Bible, something like 'Suffer the little children to come unto me for such as these belong in the kingdom of heaven'. Lisa has never forgotten these words. She is also still haunted by the blurred faces of the people who followed the coffin down the aisle.

They arrived at the graveside. Lisa was holding onto the coffin, and she just couldn't let it go. It was as though her hands had been glued onto it. As they started to lower the coffin Lisa wanted to follow it in there; she didn't want to leave Matthew… he needed his mummy. Lisa was his mummy and he needed her… and she needed him. Lisa can't remember who prised her hands off the coffin. Her grief was so overwhelming. Her tears would not stop. Her world had been turned upside down.

Although Peter and Lisa had grieved in very different ways, their pain was the same. She had trouble functioning at an everyday level, and she couldn't fathom how she had failed Matthew. At least, this was how Lisa felt – the reality was that she hadn't failed anyone. Although Peter could express his pain through anger and frustration, and by constantly questioning how this tragedy could have happened, as an Aussie male he had been brought up not to cry in public. They would go into his room every night and pray that Matthew would come back to them. Most of the time they just cried.

Lisa can't remember who prised her hands off the coffin. Her grief was so overwhelming. Her tears would not stop. Her world had been turned upside down.

Peter wanted to go down to the cemetery every day to be with Matthew, but Lisa couldn't. It was too hard for her. That was the place that had taken her son and wouldn't give him back. Instead, she would belt her fist into a pillow to express her heartache. She started waking at 3.30am each and every morning for months after Matthew's passing. The grief soon became overwhelming for both of them. They decided to go to see Peter's sister in Adelaide – she had experienced SIDS (Sudden Infant Death Syndrome) a few years before, with a baby boy who passed away at only three months of age.

SINKING

While Lisa and Peter were away in Adelaide, Lisa's mum packed up all of Matthew's things. She didn't throw them out; she just packed them up. His clothes, toys, bedding… there was so much. It was not until much later that Lisa realised how terribly hard it must have been for her to pack up Matthew's things, as he had been her first and only grandson. Lisa says, 'I am grateful to my mum for doing this, as I would not have been able to'.

Peter returned to work. Lisa was a stay-at-home mum who had lost her status as a mother; she had no one to look after now. Her life seemed to be a continuous blur. However, one day she drove through a red light at a major intersection. She then realised that she had to get help. Depression had set in from Matthew's death and it was all-encompassing. Lisa was prescribed antidepressants and stopped driving for many weeks. One day, while going through some photos, she couldn't stop crying. She knew that her regular dose of tablets wouldn't stop the crying, so in desperation she took all of them. Honestly, who would be able to think clearly in the face of such grief? If you are reading this and feeling the type of pain Lisa felt, please pick up the phone and call or text someone. Don't be alone at this time. There is help and comfort available. If you live in Australia, please call Lifeline on 13 11 14 or Beyond Blue on 1300 22 4636. If you live overseas, please Google your national crisis-support organisation.

Lisa called her doctor straight away and spoke to his receptionist. Lisa told her that the tablets weren't working. 'They haven't stopped me from crying,' she said. The receptionist asked her how many tablets she had taken. Lisa told her, 'All of them!' She was put on hold and was then told that an ambulance was on its way. Once at the hospital, they pumped her stomach and had her see a psychiatrist. She could not really say why she'd overdosed, but she did ask the psychiatrist, 'Can you give my son back?' When he said 'No', Lisa looked at him and said, 'Then you cannot help me'. I can't even begin to imagine the depth of Lisa's pain...

Lisa says, 'I had to go through the grieving process slowly – one step at a time, one day at a time'. She lost count of how often she would ring up her mum and beat herself up for what she must have missed when doing CPR. It feels as though she went over it millions of times in her head, never looking at what she may have done right; only looking for what she may have done wrong. Lisa needed answers, real answers, as to why Matthew had died. They later received his autopsy report, which told them that Matthew was a SIDS baby. He was almost 21 months old when he died, and he was one of the oldest children in Tasmania to succumb to cot death.

YET MORE TRAGEDY

At approximately 9am on 1 December 1985, just four months after Matthew's sudden death, Lisa's mum phoned to tell her that her dad had also suddenly died. He was only 59. Lisa, already overwhelmed by grief, attended her dad's funeral but found it extremely difficult to cope. She went down to stay with her mum for a few weeks and it was there she saw firsthand just how bad grief can get.

Lisa's mum would not eat or sleep. She would sit at the table and smoke, drink wine and talk. One day Lisa noticed a change in her. Lisa's mum pulled out a .22-caliber shotgun and set it on the table. She intended to shoot herself. Lisa kept saying to her, 'Please, Mum, don't do this... Please don't do this... You have your children to think of. I know you are grieving but please don't do this'. Lisa doesn't know how long her pleading continued and although her mother did not commit suicide or threaten it again, she eventually passed away from cancer in 2009.

TRYING TO MOVE ON

Peter and Lisa tried for another baby and eventually found out they were pregnant. Their daughter Natalie was born in 1987. However, it was so hard when she started school and achieved milestones that Matthew never made, as this reignited their grief. Lisa recalls, 'Milestones were always the hardest, including when the little boy across the road started school'. She often found herself wondering what Matthew would look like and what he would be doing at certain ages.

Sadly, the grief that Peter and Lisa felt was tearing them apart. Lisa says that Peter has never blamed her for Matthew's death, but as Matthew's mother, she has always felt she should have been able to save him. 'Grief does strange things to people, and we are never quite the same again.' Peter and Lisa separated in 1991, and their main concern was Natalie. They both eventually married other people, but those marriages didn't work out. Peter, though, is now happily married, and while Lisa is more than happy for him, she remains single (for now ☺). Lisa's outlook on the world has changed considerably from when she was younger. She says, 'I am more cynical. I have become more detached and find it very hard to get close to people and to trust'.

In May 2011 Lisa's brother passed away from cancer at age 49. Lisa felt overwhelmed by the memories of grief she had experienced in her home state of Tasmania – it was all becoming too much for her. So, in November 2011 she made the huge move to Townsville in Queensland. It was not a light decision. She experienced pain all over again at the thought of leaving her daughter in Tasmania. She felt so guilty, as though she was abandoning her. However, Natalie said these beautiful words to her at the airport on the day she left: 'I am so proud of you living your life, Mum'. Lisa will never forget those words. They eased the grief she had been feeling.

FAMILY LOVE

In October 2012 Natalie was married in Devonport, Tasmania, and Lisa couldn't be prouder of her. 'Her husband Iain is a beautiful, caring man who thinks the world of her,' she reflects. At the ceremony Natalie and Iain made a donation to the SIDS foundation in memory of Matthew. Natalie also released butterflies in memory of those who had passed away, and one butterfly came back and sat upon her finger. She looked at Lisa and said, 'That's Matthew, Mum'. It brought tears to Lisa's eyes... they even have a special photograph of it. In fact, you can see this special, memorable photo for yourself at the end of Lisa's story. 'My daughter is an amazing young lady who is now a mum herself and she's finding out that it's not as easy as it seems,' Lisa says. She remembers Natalie once phoning her and saying, 'Gee, Mum, being a parent is hard'. Lisa laughed at her and said, 'No s***, Sherlock!' Natalie is still finding her feet with motherhood, but she and her husband are fantastic parents.

Lisa sees Natalie and her family in person as often as she can, and flies to Tasmania each year. She has experienced major ups and downs in her life, including issues with moving homes and breaking both of her arms, yet she still tries to see the positives that life holds. Lisa says, 'Sometimes it's really hard to do this when life throws curveballs at you'. She has seen and done some amazing things in her life, but the greatest of these was becoming a mother. Although she lost a child, she has beautiful memories of him that will stay in her heart forever. From conception, a mother is always connected to her child – no matter what happens.

Peter and Lisa remain friends to this day, and neither of them will ever forget the incredible bond that they have through their deceased son and, of course, their daughter. Recently, Lisa spent Christmas with her daughter and her family, Peter and his wife, and in-laws and friends. They hired a hall, decorated it and had a wonderful Christmas Day celebration. They hope to do it again.

Lisa tries to have a video call each week with her daughter so that she can catch up with her and chat with Lisa's four-year-old granddaughter, who always likes to tell her what she is reading and playing with, how she helps Mum and Dad and how preschool is going. Lisa is learning to enjoy her life and looks forward to these special times. Her daughter, son-in-law and granddaughter are the most precious things in Lisa's life, and she makes sure to tell them that as often as possible.

HEALING HELP

Lisa's life has changed so much since that fateful day nearly 35 years ago. She says, 'There will always be a piece of my heart missing'. She also believes that although people say, 'Time heals all wounds', you never forget, but you learn to accept.

Grief-struck

Whenever she can, Lisa writes down her feelings and writes poetry. This practice has helped her to grieve, to witness her journey and to see how, over the years, she has moved from anger, frustration and sadness to acceptance. Lisa says, 'It doesn't matter if the words only make sense to you and no one else. They are yours and sometimes they will remind you of a special memory, as I have found my words so often do'.

One of Lisa's favourite quotes is by Brooke Hampton, and she would like to share it with you:

> *'I hope there are days when your coffee tastes like magic, your playlist makes you dance, strangers make you smile, and the night sky touches your soul. I hope there are days when you fall in love with being alive.'*

A final note...

Oh my goodness, you can just feel the anguish in Lisa's story. Perhaps, like me, you had tears in your eyes when you read it. I have so much empathy for Lisa and for any other women who have experienced the same situation or something similar. I have a small understanding of this because I had a stillborn son called James. At the time of writing this book he would have been 23, and Lisa's words resonate with me: 'You never forget, but you learn to accept'.

It's interesting that we can get through so much in our lives, including something as extreme as grief. It's a mere five-letter word but it packs such a punch, doesn't it? When grief strikes us, we can spiral down into a heap, and... you know what? That's OK for a season – 'It's OK to not be OK'. However, I would add, 'Let's not stay there'.

So how do you get over the grief and anguish of losing your baby? Or perhaps you've lost an older child, a partner, parents, other family members or friends?

I believe that the number one thing (although please note that I'm no expert in grief) is that you need to feel the grief. Be in the moment. Allow the grief and the tears to well up. Write about it. Take the time to remember the positives of the person you've lost. Draw strength from all of the positives and even the negatives, and allow those to help you look forward rather than dwell in the loss and the grief.

Let go of feelings of grief when they come to the surface. Take special care of yourself. There is no need to apologise for your journey. Prioritise yourself, allow yourself to LIVE your journey and just do the best you can at the time. Use the amazing gift of your imagination to rekindle dreams for your life and your future. Take your time – there is no rush. Don't be surprised if waves of grief surprise you along your journey. That's OK. Allow each feeling to be felt. Surround yourself with people who can lift you up, even when you can't lift yourself.

So often we think we have to be 'all that'. Instead, let's be *real women* – not every day is a story of peaches and cream. You really can live your best life, no matter what life throws at you. I know that Lisa is working daily on her mindset. She often shares amazing inspirational quotes on social media, and she draws her strength and hope from them. This is actually how I came across her, through her sharing of positive quotes. There is power in our words, so be inspired by Lisa and surround yourself with positive words that empower you and others around you.

I have another thought I'd like to leave with you – when you experience a loss as huge as Lisa's (and, if you recall, the initial loss of Matthew continued with the loss of her dad, then her marriage, and later her brother), you need to allow time to heal but also to create a new vision for your life. Having a life vision will enable you to get up each day with a purpose that propels you, even if you have experienced enormous anguish and grief.

Note: if you (or a loved one) is suffering from a SIDS loss, you can find support here: rednosegriefandloss.org.au.

Real Women, Real Stories

a special message from...

LISA

LYNDA BROOK

HAVE A GO – DON'T HOLD BACK!

Before we begin...

Lynda has impacted my life more than she or anyone else knows. She found my Connections Coffee'n'Chats meet-up group on the internet and, to be honest, I felt so out of my depth when I first met her. I was concerned about whether I could be of support to her – what did I have to offer? Would I be enough? We can often feel intimidated when we meet someone who is different to us and we may not know how to relate to them. What do I mean by 'different', you ask? That may not even be the right word to use, nor be the politically correct reference... but Lynda is 'different' in that she has a physical disability and is wheelchair-bound. It's important to remember, though, that there is so much that we can discover about other people, even if they do not look the same as us or act the same as us, or if they have any type of disability.

Despite my initial feelings of intimidation, Lynda always made me feel at ease. I was so honoured that she would later invite me to her home, and to her birthday parties. Why, you ask? Well, it was evident to me that Lynda was a courageous woman with such amazing insights into life. My thinking and approach to life was challenged because I started to look at all the things that I had taken for granted. Lynda is so positive and encouraging. She has kept me accountable to the dream I've had of writing this very book, and for that I'm eternally grateful. I asked her to share some of the incredible experiences she's had in her life, and I know that her story will inspire you to your very core! (By the way, Lynda has never stopped coming to Coffee'n'Chats in more than two years, and she always adds value to our conversations!)

Lynda's story

When she reflects on her life, Lynda knows that she was born at the right time, in the right season, in the right place and on purpose. There is nothing better in life than having this confidence. Some may question Lynda's positive, assured outlook on her life when they meet her and find out she has had a lifelong disability. There were many years that passed by Lynda with no answers to her symptoms, nor did she have the knowledge until later in life that she had been born with this disabling condition.

THE EARLY YEARS

When Lynda was four years of age, her mother started noticing that Lynda had extensive weight loss, and that she was falling over and losing her balance more and more often. Wondering if she was developing as a four-year-old should, Lynda's mum took her off to the doctor, who identified that Lynda was flat-footed, and that she also had 'drop foot' (meaning she had trouble lifting the front of her foot). These conditions were why Lynda fell over easily. She was soon fitted with special Clarks shoes, which were built up by a bootmaker to help with the balance issues. They were hoping this would help bring Lynda's foot back into alignment and rectify the problem. However, it didn't end up helping much at all. At this point, Lynda's disability was not identified – only basic measures were put in place to support her. She loved her pretty dainty clothes and never really noticed or cared about the shoes she was required to wear; she simply felt beautiful in her clothes.

Lynda was born at Sydney's Crown Street Women's Hospital. She grew up as a country girl in Condobolin in rural central New South Wales. Her family lived on farming properties where her parents worked very long hours. Her mum cooked and sewed, and her dad managed local farms, all to make ends meet. Lynda had two older siblings, and because she was the baby of the family she was often spoilt.

At the tender age of nine, Lynda found out through the class bully that she was adopted. At first, she didn't want to believe it. Lynda says, 'I honestly didn't understand it at all as a young girl. I didn't know what to think'. What a way to find out that you're adopted. She felt belittled and humiliated. She was so upset and confused. Her mother hadn't yet told her that they'd adopted her at five months of age; however, secrecy about adoption was the norm in those days. She had a very loving, caring, supportive and stable family environment, for which she's eternally grateful. Lynda was able to meet her biological mother once, for the first time, much later in life.

Lynda's shock at finding out she was adopted wasn't the only jigsaw she had to piece together – there were many more challenges to come. While at that point in her primary years there was no real definitive diagnosis for the physical issues she was having, she knew something clearly wasn't right. Lynda recalls, 'At times I didn't feel it was fair for me to have a physical disability, nor could I understand what was happening to me. There were no answers'.

TEENAGE LIFE

As a teenager, Lynda dealt with each day as it came while her physical challenges increased. Her mum always said, 'Lynda took things in her stride and just got on with living her life and doing exactly what the doctors told her to do, at every turn'. She always wanted to dance, run and play sports but she realised that she had to accept difficulties and certain challenges, all while trying to achieve her dreams. Her sister was a lifeline who gave her heaps of encouragement for conquering life, and her parents and friends were also incredibly supportive – Lynda had certainly been placed in the perfect supportive environment. Sometimes, depending on the situation, she struggled with feeling frustrated and emotional, but she tried to fit in as best she could. At every possible opportunity she had a determined go at life. She says, 'I believed in myself while growing up, and I didn't allow my physical disabilities to dictate my life. I was surrounded by great friends and family and this enhanced my ability to lead a fulfilling life'. Lynda had two very special friends, and the country town and atmosphere surrounding her was her saviour.

In her teens, the family moved to a small farm that was a long way from town. Initially Lynda caught the bus to school, but the trip and the long days were too tiring. Her parents wanted her to have the best schooling and opportunities, so it was decided that she would attend a Catholic boarding school in Parkes. The nuns took great care of her. Lynda recalls, 'It felt like one big family – I loved it. It was an all-girls' school, not co-ed. I created many new friendships'.

Her physical disability meant she faced many different challenges. She used one crutch to support herself while she walked along, hanging on tightly to handrails. Climbing steps took extra energy and time. Lynda often left earlier than her peers to arrive at meals and school classes; this allowed her the time and space to get there without crowds of students pushing around her. She still wore her strong, built-up Clarks school shoes, but she was also consistently wearing splints. These were made from strong plastic and were fitted inside her shoes – they helped regulate her walking and balance. She began to encounter more weakening in her legs and hands and became very concerned that her physical abilities were changing for the worse.

LEAVING HOME

Lynda finished boarding school at the end of year 10 and moved to Mt Wilga Private Rehabilitation Centre in Sydney. She was 16 years of age, and by this stage it was becoming clearer to see what support she would need to cope with her disabilities. The centre helped young people with physical disabilities to become more independent, offering them training for various jobs so that they could find employment. Staff also helped with the development of everyday life skills, including managing money, grocery shopping, cooking and general self-care. She made the decision to train to become a telephonist. A mere 12 months later, Lynda landed a job at Kings Cross Hotel, where she did shift work as a telephonist.

She really loved the job, but it did make her quite tired. By this time her sister was living in Darlinghurst, so Lynda moved into the flat with her and her partner for a while. Lynda now felt that there was a brighter future ahead of her. She was at the age where she could make her own decisions and finally take responsibility for her own path in life.

From her young teens, Lynda has always had a strong, determined personality and an optimistic attitude. Finding her place in life and pushing her capabilities were always top of mind. She was determined to fulfil her full potential – to follow her passions, try new things and meet new people. As she moved through her teens, she slowly matured and learned how to express her needs, although living with a physical disability in the big smoke was no easy feat.

A DIAGNOSIS

In 1976, Lynda was admitted to the Royal Prince Alfred Hospital in Sydney. She had been feeling weaker, and was going downhill, physically. At the time, she was still living independently with her sister in Sydney, and it was her sister who had encouraged her to seek help. After seeing countless doctors and receiving no answers, she was finally referred to the hospital's head professor of neurology. The professor performed a nerve biopsy on Lynda's leg, and this revealed that she had a genetic condition called Charcot-Marie-Tooth. This is a rare degenerative neuromuscular condition that weakens a person's extremities and affects the mobility of the rest of the body. The doctors explained that in order for this condition to have been passed on, her mother and father would have to have carried the gene. However, because she was adopted, she had no way of tracing this back.

Lynda felt such relief at receiving a diagnosis after so many years of searching – until that point the search had involved long hospital stays, extensive and invasive medical testing, and surgical procedures. Finally, she had a name for her condition. As she listened intently to what the doctors were telling her, overwhelming feelings started to engulf her. She wondered what all of this would mean for her in the future.

In the months following the diagnosis, Lynda slowly faced many realisations. It took her a while to comprehend how this was going to impact her life. Because there was no cure for her condition, she knew she would need to be in the medical system for the rest of her life. Things were not necessarily going to be easy, and she would continue to be challenged by her condition on a daily basis.

HAPPY YEARS AHEAD

City life took its mental and physical toll on Lynda, so she escaped back to her parents for a break. Eventually, at age 22, she moved to the beautiful sunny town of Coffs Harbour with her friend Kerry, with the aim of making a fresh start. Lynda soon found herself some casual employment at a preschool.

One night, after several months of living in Coffs Harbour, Lynda met a terrific sweet man. She fell very much in love with this wonderful person, and he literally swept her off her feet. After two years of dating, she finally had the opportunity to become a bride. Her family were all supportive of her decision to marry him. Lynda felt as though her wedding was a fairytale. They married on a late summer's afternoon in a beautiful park featuring a central fountain and shady trees. The majority of her family members, relatives and friends attended, which was so exciting. Lynda says, 'I woke up every morning for weeks thinking, "I am getting married and I'm going to be his wife" – I couldn't believe it'. Her mother was her supporter and saviour – she made the wedding dress, helped with all the arrangements, organised flowers and wrote invitations. That summer day was absolutely magical. 'It was the best day of my life,' she says. 'Dad was all smiles giving me away.'

Lynda felt totally exhilarated that her dream of being a wife had come true – and her next dream was to have children. She believed that being a wife and mother was her real life purpose, but the doctors had said, 'No babies!' They didn't believe Lynda would have the strength to sustain a pregnancy. She had retorted, 'Watch me!' and went on to prove them wrong.

She couldn't believe that her dream for children came true, despite all the odds. Lynda gave birth to two daughters, and they felt like an absolute blessing from God. It was such a miracle to have her own little family. Lynda had four pregnancies in total, but had two miscarriages between the births of her eldest daughter Candice and her second daughter Kylie.

IT ALL BECOMES HARDER

It was during her second pregnancy that Lynda started to lose her physical strength. She felt constantly tired and had lots of falls, and she worried that she'd either hurt the baby or herself. So, she made the decision to succumb to the assistance of a manual wheelchair. Not long after, she moved into an electric wheelchair. However, she was not happy about using a wheelchair and desperately kept trying to use just a single crutch! Although she hated her chair, it was necessary. It was around this time that the realisation of her disability set in even more, and life became more difficult. It was possible that Lynda's condition worsened because of the pregnancies and later relationship stresses. Although her condition also plateaued at times, she felt something like a battery-operated toy... she was no longer the rabbit bouncing around with energy; instead, she was slowing down as her batteries gradually become flat.

Have a Go – Don't Hold Back!

Unexpectedly, after 10 years of feeling happily married, things changed for Lynda and her husband. They started to experience many different issues – including a lack of communication, money problems and an inability to compromise – and these caused them to drift apart. Their marriage started to break down. They tried several ways to make the marriage work, but they didn't have the strategy or tools needed to fix it. Eventually, they separated, and Lynda made the decision to leave New South Wales and move to Cairns in northern Queensland. Cairns was appealing for its warmer weather, and because two of Lynda's friends lived there. She soon realised that she'd be a single mother, living by herself with her two daughters in a new place. She would have no family living close by, and needed to rely on herself, carers and friends to support her needs and help to look after her young daughters. The decision to move away took a lot of courage.

By now, Lynda was now fairly wheelchair-bound and needed wheelchair accommodation. However, this was very difficult to find, and the search for adequate housing caused her to struggle immensely, especially because she was receiving very little financial assistance. She and her girls were living on government benefits, but this was not nearly enough to pay for typical rental properties. After staying with friends for a few months, they ended up staying in a women's shelter for several more months while they waited for Department of Housing accommodation to be approved.

While they waited for a home of their own, Lynda felt totally devastated, broken-hearted, angry and depressed. She felt as though she had failed her daughters by not being able to provide a home and the security they needed. With a lot of support and counselling and by making new friends, Lynda eventually pulled herself out of that dark hole.

Finally, the Department found them a unit to call home. Life started to look a lot brighter. At this time, Lynda's girls were still quite young and were very excited to move into their new home. The little family trio gradually settled into their new life. However, although they made it their home for several years, the area they were living in became increasingly less suitable. They experienced house break-ins and vandalism, and this made Lynda feel uneasy and unsafe, especially because she was a single mother in a wheelchair raising two children.

Although she and her girls had had six interesting years in Cairns, a decision was eventually made by the Department to build her a four-bedroom, wheelchair-accessible home in Townsville (a four-hour drive south of Cairns). It also had a yard for her children to play in, which would be wonderful after so many years of living in a unit. Townsville's climate was appealing to Lynda, and it was also affordable and there were opportunities for the girls. By 1996, their new home was ready for them, so Lynda and her daughters made the move.

THE TOWNSVILLE TRANSITION

Despite now having a purpose-built home, Lynda thought to herself, 'Oh my God, how did we get here and what am I doing?' Here she was in an unfamiliar city, with no connections, no plans and no certainty for their futures. She felt so scared. 'How am I ever going to make this work and be a good mum?' she asked herself.

Feelings of emptiness and despair kept pressing on her, and her life felt like a jigsaw, with many pieces of it missing. She felt scattered and overwhelmed, and although she wanted more for herself and her children, she felt clueless about where to start. 'I definitely didn't know what I was supposed to do,' she says.

Have a Go – Don't Hold Back!

After a while, Lynda realised that her daughters were settling well into their new town and school and were making new friends. Both girls were becoming more independent, especially when they started high school (which was not long after the move). During this season of life, they were a very close family unit. Candice, Lynda's firstborn, was her rock. She says, 'My family and children had a huge influence on my life, and I found motherhood to be incredibly rewarding'. However, although she loved being a mum, she also desperately wanted to know what else she was meant to be doing with her life. She was trying to find her niche, and always felt as though she was taking very slow steps forward. However, at least this was better than going backwards – that was not in her life plan. Lynda decided that if she could make more money to help with everyday living, this would at least be some type of goal she'd like to achieve!

OPPORTUNITIES ABOUND

Sitting outside on a Saturday afternoon in 1999, Lynda asked herself, 'Is this really my life? How did I get here and what am I supposed to do next?' She was now 40 years of age and had two daughters who needed her. Being a single mother was not easy, and she felt lonely, fearful and inadequate. She wondered what her life would have been like if she hadn't moved interstate, if she had had a better education, if her marriage had not broken up, if she wasn't a working mother (she had been working as a teacher aide) and if she had had no disability to hold her back. However, she knew this was not the reality of her story. On that day she made a conscious decision not to stay mired in negativity and fear, and instead to find her purpose and pursue it.

Over the next several years, Lynda set about creating new opportunities, meeting people and developing friendships.

She volunteered as a facilitator at Spinal Life Australia. In that role, she worked as a disability advocate within the community, facilitated member network meetings and helped organise social events (ensuring they were held in accessible areas). Lynda made connections and lifelong friendships that she cherishes. She is still a member of Spinal Life Australia, and she really appreciates that it has expanded her knowledge and understanding of a diverse range of physical disabilities. This voluntary work helped open windows of opportunities for Lynda, ones that she hadn't even known existed.

Through her volunteering work, and chats with her dear friend Genevieve, Lynda realised she had a passion for becoming a disability counsellor – and that this was something that had always been in her. However, when it came to deciding on whether to study for a diploma, there were many things to weigh up. How would it benefit her family? How would she cope? How would she find the time to study *and* raise teenage daughters? 'I kept questioning whether I was capable of chasing my dream, and I prayed to God for answers.' Before she knew it, she had completed the 12-month course.

She felt ecstatic at having achieved such a special goal. Hard work, and long hours of training and typing, had paid off. Lynda was starting to feel as though anything was possible. She felt so encouraged and knew that her daughters were proud of her. Lynda says, 'I was also proud of myself'. Graduation night, with all her fellow students, was so special. She was dressed in a beautiful long black evening dress, and had her hair and make-up done – this made her feel complete. A journalist from the *Townsville Bulletin* was there on the night to write a short story in honour of her success, and while this was exciting, Lynda was full of mixed emotions. She didn't know what to expect from the story (she needn't have worried!) or from the evening as a

How would she find the time to study and raise teenage daughters? 'I kept questioning whether I was capable of chasing my dream, and I prayed to God for answers.' Before she knew it, she had completed the 12-month course.

whole, nor did she know what to expect from the next chapter of her life. However, Lynda's daughters and special friend Genevieve (the friend who had encouraged her to undertake studies in the first place) were there to celebrate graduation night with her, so she let herself relax and enjoy it all.

LIFE WITH AN EXTRA CHALLENGE

Lynda is often asked about her daily life, with people wondering what challenges she faces (and has faced in the past) as a person with a disability. She chooses not to be defined by her chair, saying, 'I do not live my life focused on what I cannot do. Instead, I focus on what I can do, and I challenge myself continually'. A recent challenge has included sharing her story with us, in this book – and that was no mean feat! (I'm also SO grateful that she wouldn't let me lay down my dream for this book.) She is such an inspiration, and once you catch a glimpse of the challenges she faces in her everyday life, I know you'll feel empowered to face any challenge in your life, too.

Lynda's typical day is 10 times harder to deal with than a person who does not have a disability. When you are wheelchair-bound, moving out of your chair is not easy. When you don't have a disability, you undertake everyday actions automatically and easily – you get up out of bed, you sit in a lounge chair, you shower, you use the toilet, you jump in the car and off you go… well, it's not so easy for Lynda.

Each day, she wakes at around 8am. She sleeps in a queen-sized bed with a firm mattress, as this gives her body the support it needs for movement and transfers. An electric wheelchair is positioned next to her bed. To move onto the chair, she lifts herself across using foot plates and by supporting herself with her right arm. Lynda slides across into the chair, and this process uses most of her upper-body strength. She says, 'For me, the process for transferring to a wheelchair is the same mobility transfer I use for the toilet, and the shower bench in the bathroom'.

So, what happens when Lynda goes out in a car? She says, 'My transfer into a low car is a similar process; however, with assistance from a carer I am able to slide across from my electric wheelchair into the front passenger seat, using a transfer slide board'. The carer then moves the wheelchair into the garage at the front of the house, and folds and places Lynda's manual wheelchair into the car for using while they are out and about. Her manual chair has been custom-made to suit her needs. The framework is ultra light, which means it can be lifted easily by Lynda's personal carers, who are women. It has quick-release wheels and an adjustable backrest that fits comfortably. She uses pressure cushions on both wheelchairs, and these are prescribed professionally by an occupational therapist. Lynda says, 'These cushions prevent pressure areas due to lack of my mobility. Assessments on my equipment are done regularly and vary each year due to the decline in my physical condition'. How wonderful that products and services like these are available!

Lynda has five carers who work in regular shifts. They attend to her every day in her home, and help her with meal preparation (when the carers are not there, Lynda will heat the meals or prepare them herself), cleaning, gardening, laundry, her personal care and the regular walking of Ellie, her companion dog. She employs the carers through her NDIS (National Disability Insurance Scheme) funding. The NDIS has provided a yearly funding package over the past three years, and although the management of her funding comes with its own set of headaches, it has been a godsend.

Lynda likes to keep busy. Just a few of her activities include social outings such as 10-pin bowling, shopping, our Coffee'n'Chats meet-ups, and doing craft. She loves costume dress-ups and is known for her Halloween costume parties and themed birthday gatherings. She also has physiotherapy appointments – these are important for retaining her upper-body strength, which enables Lynda to keep some of her independence.

In the evening, Lynda rests, visits websites such as dailyom.com, watches movies and listens to inspirational podcasts (she has a love of personal development). She always has music playing and she loves Celine Dion. She says, 'Music calms me and helps me to relax'.

THE FULL & HAPPY LIFE

In recent times, Lynda's health has deteriorated further, with yet more nerve damage. She will most likely use morphine patches for the rest of her life. However, she still has the ability to smile in the face of adversity, and to choose to think beyond her circumstances to live a full life.

A lovely man called Errol came into Lynda's world during the writing of this story, and he has contributed to her life in so many positive ways. He is the best man she's ever met, and she never imagined she would meet someone like him later in life. Lynda says, 'I believe God sent Errol to me to be a part of my life, to be the icing on the cake and to fulfil my dreams of reaching the sky'. Errol has received the stamp of approval from her daughters, and they don't hold back when it comes to their mum's love life!

Lynda lives in a wheelchair-accessible two-bedroom unit, and she has so much support and is so engaged in life. Errol lives only about an hour away and often comes to stay. Her daughters and their families live nearby, and she adores having sleepover visits from her grandchildren. Also, she loves the companionship of Ellie, her 12-year-old Staffordshire terrier. Ellie is a rescue dog and is very obedient, loyal and well-mannered, with a lovely nature. Lynda has trained her to be incredibly conscious of her wheelchair – she is aware that she cannot jump up and hurt Lynda's legs. She has adapted incredibly well to Lynda's needs, realising that she has a physical disability.

HAVE A GO!
Given the challenges she's faced in her life, Lynda could easily be an unhappy and negative person. However, she has chosen not to let fear rule her life. She says, 'Don't let things stop you. Fear has not stopped me. Of course, I have some fears, but fear doesn't drive me and dictate my life any more than this chair does! If I can face my fears and have a go, *you* can'.

Even though she gets to choose her attitude to life, sometimes she encounters resistance from people without disability who think she isn't capable of doing things, just because she has a disability. She says, 'Don't say "No" to me because you see my chair, and don't overlook me. I have a feisty personality, so if you say "No", I'll say "Let me show you!"'

Lynda makes the most of her abilities and counts every day as a blessing. Her faith and beliefs keep her going, and she has made a conscious choice to see her challenges as opportunities. 'It's not my disability; it's my ability to have a go!'

A final note...

Wow, what an absolutely incredible life story – and I know there is so much more detail we could go into.

You know, Lynda has ups and downs, just like the rest of us. However, the thing that strikes me most about her story is that she has chosen not to let her circumstances define her. Lynda is not the sum total of her adoption at five months, nor is she the sum total of what her chair allows her to do. She has not allowed these limitations to determine who she is.

So often, we choose to let our circumstances take over and define who we are. However, we can also choose to be defined by the person we *want* to become. 'But Jen,' you say, 'you don't know my story'. No, maybe I don't, and I'm well aware that we are all different, but one thing I do know is that *you* get to decide.

You choose to allow your circumstances to hold you back – or not. You can choose to do things that limit you, or things that propel you forward. The choice is completely yours. I often used to say, 'I don't have a choice. What can I do? I'm powerless to change this!' However, those thoughts were all lies. I had those lies on replay in my head, and perhaps you do, too! We can say instead, 'I do have a choice. I can change things. I can have a go, and I will'. It's up to you!

Take on board Lynda's advice: 'I do not live my life focused on what I cannot do. Instead, I focus my life on what I can do, and I challenge myself continually'.

You choose!

Have a Go – Don't Hold Back!

a special message from...

LYNDA

VERONICA ROSE*

Please note that all names have been changed throughout this story

RED FLAGS

Before we begin...

I met beautiful Veronica during Easter of 2006, at a church service on the Sunshine Coast. She had lived a full life, having had a successful career in banking and travel prior to children, but in 2005 she went through a divorce. After this she was ready to pursue new experiences, and she wanted a life that included God and a church community. At the time, I was also a single mum and ran a 'Significant Singles' group and a 'Divorce Care' workshop within the church and for the non-church community. Over time, Veronica and I became great friends. We both had two boys each of similar ages, we both faced similar struggles and we both wanted more for our lives. Veronica has encountered many challenges in her life, yet she has always had an amazing optimistic attitude. She has even inspired me to lighten up a little! However, so many of her challenges pale in comparison to her recent journey. Let me share Veronica's precious story with you – even if you have never received a serious health diagnosis (and hopefully never will), Veronica will inspire you to get through any adversity.

Veronica's story

In November 2004, at the age of 49, Veronica found herself divorced with two young boys. She had left her marriage without any financial security... absolutely none. Financial security was so important to her, as it is for any woman, of any age, who is facing life as a single mother. Her 50th birthday was only seven months away, and it was a reminder that she was having to virtually 'start again' later in life and without a financial footing. Veronica has lived on Queensland's beautiful Sunshine Coast since 2001, but was originally from Sydney – so for her special birthday she had planned a Sydney-based party, as well as a local party. The interstate event would be for her family, childhood friends and her sons' playgroup friends, and the local celebration would be for the large community of new friends she had made on the Coast. Both of these events would be fabulous and she was looking forward to celebrating. There is nothing Veronica loves more than a good party and celebrating with loved ones. She chose not to let the impact of divorce and financial uncertainty dampen the celebrations of not only her 50th birthday but of her new-found single life.

However, about three months before her birthday, she started noticing some memory loss and other strange, reoccurring health issues. For example, she would go to the supermarket with her list (yes, she is a list person) yet forget to buy some items from it. Also, her period had changed drastically, from two to three days of light bleeding to seven days of heavy, so she booked in to see a menopause doctor. Do take note here – these were the first red flags Veronica experienced. So often we ignore changes to our bodies. I'm so glad Veronica quickly made a doctor's appointment.

Red Flags

THE LUMP

Veronica's family had a history of cancer – her brother had experienced testicular cancer, and her sister and mother had had breast cancer (diagnosed within 72 hours of each other in 2000). Whenever there is a known history of cancer in a family, doctors test fairly rigorously, no matter the symptoms. The menopause doctor gave Veronica a thorough examination and referred her for a mammogram. The good news was that her symptoms were typical of perimenopause, and she could take natural HRT for a very short period of time (until the symptoms settled down). Veronica was relieved that there was a reason for her foggy memory, and was glad that her periods would become more regular. What a relief this must have been!

The very next morning, Veronica headed to the shops – with her list at the ready – after dropping her boys at their bus stop. However, on the drive she felt pain under her right armpit. She felt it and realised there was a small lump! She'd never had one previously and thought, 'How weird'. It seemed especially strange considering she had been examined the day before. She dismissed it, thinking, 'Oh well, it must have flared up with all the probing around'. By the end of her shopping trip, that lump had become more painful. Veronica put her groceries into the car and proceeded to the ladies' toilets. She rolled up her top and saw in the mirror a visible, red pea-sized lump that was very sore when she touched it and around it. This sounds like another red flag!

Returning to her car, Veronica decided to ring the menopause doctor to see whether or not she should go back in. The receptionist asked Veronica to hold while she spoke to the doctor. Veronica kept thinking of the saying, 'If you have a lump that is sore you have nothing to worry about – it's the ones without pain you need to be concerned about'. The receptionist came back on the line and said that they had just had a cancellation and that she should come straight in.

Veronica hurriedly pulled up at the surgery with her groceries still in the car, worrying that they were going to spoil if all of this took a while. She tried not to think too much about why she had a lump, but she was curious about what could be going on. Soon she was chatting away to the receptionist, noting that she hadn't expected to be back there just one day after her appointment! The doctor was also surprised that Veronica had a lump, because she had done a thorough search of the lymph nodes the day before. She said, 'I'll send you off for an ultrasound and once we have the results of both your mammogram and ultrasound, we'll take it from there'.

The ultrasound appointment was made for two days' time, and on the day after that Veronica would be flying interstate and enjoying the fun and frivolity of the first weekend of her birthday celebrations. She couldn't wait to be up, up and away from the medical madness.

AN APPOINTMENT WITH A STAPLER

After seeing the menopause doctor to have the lump checked out that morning, the pain continued all day long. At times, it made her movements difficult, such as when she brought in groceries or took the washing off the line. She had never had that type of pain before, and she hoped it would disappear quickly.

The next morning, Veronica noticed that the lump was gone. There was no sign of it, and no more pain. 'That's odd,' she thought. She considered cancelling the ultrasound, but she was so busy packing for the weekend and doing single mum duties that she didn't get around to it.

She went for the mammogram that day, and there was no comment made that led her to feel concerned. However, two days later she was having the ultrasound and the radiologist said, 'Oh, I'd better get a second opinion'.

'What?!' Veronica exclaimed. The radiologist then said, 'I'm sure it's nothing – I just need to check it'. Veronica said, 'OK,' but was thinking to herself, 'How bizarre! This is so strange'.

Minutes later, another radiologist arrived and checked her breast.

'Mmm,' said the radiologist. 'There seem to be a few small lumps around your right breast. I'm sure it's fine. However, you may need a needle biopsy to confirm that they are clear... sometimes these can be cysts and it's best to check.'

'OK,' Veronica said. Again, she thought the whole situation was odd, but she wasn't too concerned.

The next morning, she headed off to the biopsy appointment (despite having the flight booked for that afternoon) and found herself unprepared for the discomfort involved.

'My breast was stretched under a plate, almost flattening it. I had to remain still while the biopsies were taken, and this was even more uncomfortable than having a mammogram,' Veronica recalls. 'It was slightly painful to have a stapler-type machine puncture your breast a few times – and it even sounded like a stapler.'

The nurse warned Veronica that she would be quite bruised. 'Well, she wasn't wrong there,' Veronica says. She asked the staff if they would show her the biopsies, and assured them that she loved medical TV shows and wasn't squeamish about blood. So, they showed her a sample. It was like a small, slim red slug. After the procedure, Veronica picked up the boys early from school and went home to get ready for their afternoon flight to Sydney.

CARPE DIEM! (SEIZE THE DAY!)

The day after she arrived in Sydney, Veronica's mobile phone rang from an unidentified number. It was her GP, asking her to come in ASAP. Veronica said, 'Unfortunately, I can't come for another week because I'm interstate'. She asked if all was OK and was told that the biopsy showed there were suspicious cells. While she felt alarmed, she'd made a decision not to spend time worrying about things she couldn't change. She was choosing to live in the moment and didn't want to deal with it at that time. 'Oh well. I'll find out on my return,' she thought to herself.

Veronica went into the kitchen after the call and joined her mother and sister. She calmly told them the news and could see from the looks on their faces that they were thinking, 'Oh no – not you, too'. Veronica chose again to put aside the news and face the situation once she'd returned from all of her birthday celebrations. She was determined not to put a dampener on her celebrations, nor to worry her family or friends until she knew more. Veronica was in no real hurry to know. 'I'm a party person,' she says, and that was her immediate focus. It's important to note that Veronica wasn't in denial – she chose instead to live in the moment and not to dwell on things she couldn't change.

Just as she had hoped, Veronica's party was fantastic – so many friends and family came, and it was such a happy occasion.

She and her boys flew home on the Sunday afternoon, and she spent the next week excitedly immersed in preparations for the second party – shopping, cooking and setting it all up. As mentioned in the introduction to this story, Veronica started attending church (and became a Christian) when she separated from her husband, and the friendships she'd developed in her home group had provided incredible support since that time. Many of her church friends came to the party, which was a great success – it provided Veronica with so many fond memories. She couldn't believe she'd reached this milestone in her life. Time had flown by so quickly!

THE PARTY'S OVER

In the following week she was still basking in the afterglow of the celebrations when her GP rang to say, 'I'm sorry, but you will need to get a referral to see a surgeon'. WHAT? Veronica went to the GP for the referral but couldn't comprehend why she would need to see a surgeon – looking back now, she can see that she probably felt that way because she was in shock. The next week she arrived for her appointment with the prominent surgeon. Oddly, when he called Veronica in, he also asked, 'Are you alone?' Veronica's reply was, 'Yes, I am,' and she thought, 'Ah, "der"! Obviously, I am alone – when I booked my appointment no one suggested that I needed anyone here!' The surgeon drew a picture of her right breast with multiple lumps in it and explained that she had DCIS – ductal carcinoma in situ, stage 3. Now, just to explain this briefly – DCIS is considered to be pre-cancer of the breast. It is not life-threatening but could develop into an invasive cancer and possibly spread out of the ducts into other tissues. At stage 3, the cells grow quickly.

Veronica had expected him to say that she would need a lumpectomy (which is what her sister and mother had had) and to start treatment. Imagine her shock when he said, 'Unfortunately, due to having multiple lumps and with your family history, I would recommend you have a mastectomy'. (He made no mention of needing a bilateral mastectomy, which involves the removal of both breasts.)

'What?!' Veronica immediately exclaimed. 'No, I'm happy to have chemo and radiation instead.' She couldn't believe her diagnosis was as serious as it was. The doctor also said it was very fortunate that it had been discovered at that point, because if it had been left undiagnosed for another six months she could have been facing a very different situation. However, she needed to have this operation as soon as possible. He was going on holidays for one month at the end of the week and was keen to book her in to have the procedure on his return. The doctor also recommended that she go straight to the local Cancer Council branch and speak with a particular person there who would be a great support and give her excellent material about the procedure. Veronica drove straight there, reeling in shock.

The lady was available to see her and when Veronica told her of the diagnosis, she said, 'You are very lucky'. Veronica recalls thinking, 'I know it is just DCIS, but I didn't realise that losing your breast would be considered lucky!' She was given lots of reading material and a fat roll of cotton wadding with which to fill her bra after the removal of her breast. (OMG! Can you even begin to imagine being given a wad of cotton in exchange for your breast? I'm holding onto my breasts right now! Are you, too?) It felt surreal. Veronica just couldn't believe that she needed the procedure, so she decided to seek a second opinion about her diagnosis.

SECOND OPINION

About a week after seeing the first surgeon, Veronica headed off to the second surgeon, who said, 'Unfortunately, I have to agree with your last surgeon's advice'.

'Are you kidding?' Veronica exclaimed. This seemed just like a nightmare. She had thought she would just receive treatment, not lose her breast!

Veronica asked two questions:

1. Can DCIS spread to the other breast, even after the affected breast has been removed?
2. If so, would it be safer to have both breasts removed at the same time?

The surgeon advised that, in some cases, DCIS can occur in the non-removed breast, and it would therefore be wise to have both removed.

The surgeon then asked about Veronica's current relationship situation, to which she replied, 'I'm single, divorced and not in a good way financially'. The surgeon mentioned that she wanted to see if she could help her in some way, but Veronica didn't know what she meant by this.

At this stage, Veronica felt quite vulnerable, yet so respected and cared for. Within just a few weeks, her menopause doctor, GP and two surgeons had helped uncover a serious health issue that could now be treated – and all because she had followed her intuition about the early menopause symptoms and the painful lump (a lump that had disappeared within 24 hours). Talk about paying attention to RED FLAGS!

A GUARDIAN ANGEL

The following week the second surgeon rang and said, 'Hi Veronica – I have great news. You can have this complete procedure, including breast reconstruction, covered by the Raelene Boyle Foundation'. (Raelene Boyle is a retired Australian athlete who won silver medals in sprinting at the Olympic Games.) Veronica was absolutely dumbfounded, because she knew that she would not otherwise have been able to have a reconstruction – it would have cost her $12,000 to $15,000, and this was well out of her reach! Raelene didn't usually know who had received funding from her foundation; however, after the surgery Veronica was able to phone her and thank her personally. At the time of the call, Raelene was on the steps of Australia's parliament, no less! Veronica also left a personal note at Raelene's partner's café, which was located on the Sunshine Coast, thanking her for the blessing of the breast reconstruction.

HELLO, DOLLY

Three weeks after receiving that second opinion, both of Veronica's breasts were removed, including her nipples. Everything happened so fast; it was like a whirlwind. She wanted to become a Dolly Parton (ie, to go from a small B cup to a C cup) through the breast reconstruction but was told that it wouldn't be possible. 'Bugger!' Veronica thought. I remember Veronica telling me this at the time, and we laughed about it. However, I couldn't fathom how she was feeling inside.

Veronica's boys were overseas with their dad for one week during that time. Her mum flew up from Sydney a week beforehand and would stay to help her at home. Veronica recalls that her mum was an immense support to her, in every way. The outpouring of love and support from her family and friends was immeasurable.

The morning of Veronica's operation arrived. She and her mum drove to a local hospital for her iodine injection and markings, and then headed to the hospital where she would be having the operation. Veronica knew a woman called Emily who worked at the hospital, and Emily offered to escort her and her mum to the pre-op room – an offer she accepted. She then kissed her mum goodbye and went into the pre-op room with Emily.

Veronica says, 'I started getting emotional about my breasts and nipples being removed. I was thinking, "Will they be thrown in the rubbish bin? Will they be thrown into a garbage bag, where some stray dog or cat will get in and eat them?"'

She started to cry, and said to Emily, 'Could you please take photos of my breasts before they are cut off? I want to remember them'.

The history of Veronica's two breasts was about to be removed. Veronica had special memories: 'My breasts growing big enough to fill my first bra... perky enough to wear a bathing suit that enhanced them... wearing dresses and tops with confidence in my femininity... two breasts that had been part of me becoming a woman and sharing them with my lovers and then husband... breastfeeding my two boys'. She didn't realise how much emotion would rise within her, knowing that she would come out with scars across her chest and no nipples. I just can't begin to imagine the feelings Veronica would have felt, and I don't think any of us could unless we have also experienced this journey.

Veronica came to in the recovery room and was told that her surgery had been successful and that she wouldn't require radiation. This was great news! Implants had been inserted during the operation, and these would help in the creation of her new breasts. She felt a tightness in her chest, and slightly uncomfortable at the point where drains came out of the breasts, but she experienced no pain.

On the first night in hospital, the whole home group from church came to visit. She was overwhelmed by their love, support and prayers. Veronica will always be so grateful for the many people who came around her at that time.

Veronica stayed in hospital for seven nights. Upon arriving home, she was surprised by a secret bedroom makeover from some special friends. They had transformed her bedroom into a calming, loving environment. Again, she felt so much gratitude for the kindness of friends. A couple of days after Veronica was discharged her boys returned home from their overseas holiday, and she was so happy to see them.

BEST-LAID PLANS

The plan was for Veronica's mum to stay for a fortnight to help in her recovery, and then for two close friends from Sydney to come up for a week each, one after the other. This would allow her mum to return to Sydney to look after her dad, who had hurt his back. Her mum would come back up later.

However, plans can change! Unfortunately, both friends received tragic news at the last minute and weren't able to come to Veronica's house. They were distraught at not being able to help their beloved friend. Veronica completely understood their situation, but it did mean that she was left without any of the pre-planned help she so badly needed to ensure her recovery.

Veronica says, 'I then probably started to do a little too much, such as hanging out washing – this was a "no-no". Lifting your arms above your shoulders was not a good thing, and trying to hang heavy wet towels and sheets was practically impossible'. As a result of overdoing it, Veronica became anaemic. She needed to have weekly iron infusions for seven weeks. Veronica wasn't able to drive so she relied on friends to take her shopping or to doctors' appointments, and she was so grateful for the meals that were dropped off.

A couple of weeks after the operation, Veronica reflected on the reality of not having a partner to go through this journey with her. She says, 'I had no one to lay with, no one to hold me and tell me that I was still loved and attractive

On the first night in hospital, the whole home group from church came to visit. She was overwhelmed by their love, support and prayers.

to them'. It was a long, painful process for her to accept that she would do this journey without an intimate partner by her side, and she wondered if she would ever have that type of support and love again.

THE PAIN OF RECOVERY

Over the course of three years, Veronica underwent three procedures – the first, the removal of her breasts and the insertion of implants; the second, the realignment of her left breast (performed before the implants were fully pumped up, because her left breast had been extremely painful – it had moved south-west and needed to be realigned); and the third, the nipple reconstruction. In Veronica's eyes, the nipple reconstruction was a mistake.

She explains, 'You have choices with new nipples: prosthetic nipples, tattooed nipples or nipples re-created from your own skin, which in my case was to be taken from my labia'. The labia is nearly identical in colour to the areola. Extra skin is also grafted so that the nipple can be attached. Unfortunately, she says, '... although I wanted "high beam", I got "low beam"'. Also, after the nipple reconstruction Veronica couldn't wear underpants for some time because their seams cut into the graft area and caused pain. Urinating was excruciating. The 'vag' didn't look the same, and the stitches on both sides of the opening felt strange, as though they replicated the stitches of an old-fashioned cricket ball. Also, the pain was more than she expected, so she took painkillers and applied creams and moved to antidepressants to reduce nerve pain. Eventually, the pain started reducing. Mind you, the process was slow!

Veronica says, 'My breasts are both hard and rippled. My left breast has again gone south-west, and the cavity between the breasts is more prominent'. She had thought previously that she would never need to have her breasts replaced.

However, she now knows that implants are usually replaced every 10 years. She says, 'I will have them replaced one day'.

When Veronica was experiencing that severe pain after her nipple reconstruction, she stopped feeling as though she was even a woman. She would say to friends, 'Who would want me now? I'm divorced, with no financial security, and my two areas of femininity have been changed and scarred'. It took over nine years before Veronica was pain free 'down below'. The procedure using labial skin for nipple reconstructions is rarely offered now, and I can understand why!

HOPES FOR LOVE

In 2016 Veronica started opening up her heart and mind to the idea that love could be possible for her in the future. She had not gone on a date in 13 years, and it felt nice to grow into a space where she had accepted herself 'as is' and was open to meeting someone who could potentially be her future husband. What a journey of acceptance Veronica has had to endure. I think this could make us all more aware of how we should love ourselves and be grateful for our femininity as it is!

Veronica's prayer was that she wouldn't be rejected by a man once he saw her physically. She began to question, from her Christian perspective, whether or not she should have a sexual relationship with a man once she felt that he would be her lifetime partner. She felt she'd rather know before she got married whether or not her potential husband was someone who could cope with her disfigurement. Veronica says, 'I see myself getting remarried and I have so much love to give. Sometimes I've thought that the only men who may fully accept me are those who have lost a previous wife to ill health or had a family member go through the same procedures'.

ALL IN THE FAMILY

Most of Veronica's immediate family members have been touched by cancer. As mentioned earlier, Veronica's mother and sister were both diagnosed with breast cancer back in 2000. Veronica's mum also had bowel cancer in 2019, and only six months later was diagnosed with breast cancer (in the other breast). She had the breast removed and was fitted with a chemo port in the chest. She will be having regular four-hour chemotherapy sessions for some months. She is 84 years of age.

Veronica's sister has had breast cancer return, along with lymphoma in her eyelid (a very rare form of cancer). Pre-cancerous cells were also found in her uterus, resulting in a full hysterectomy. She is an incredible person and is Veronica's hero. Veronica's brother was first in the family to have experienced cancer – he had testicular cancer, but he was incredibly brave throughout and went on to have two children. This was no mean feat, and Veronica is so proud of him.

When Veronica was diagnosed with DCIS in 2006, their family went through genetic counselling. Essentially, this is where the women in the family who have had breast or ovarian cancer provide a blood sample for DNA testing. The doctors are looking for a genetic fault, and testing can take several months. If you or your family are facing the possibilities of these cancers, it's worth looking into the testing because there are preventative measures you can take. Head to the canceraustralia.gov.au website (search for the 'Genetic testing for breast/ovarian cancer risk' page) for more information. Genetic testing is offered only through a family cancer clinic.

Veronica's family doesn't have the BRCA1 or BRCA2 gene, and they were told that it was just bad luck that four people out of their family of five had gone through cancer and pre-cancerous conditions. However, genetics has come a long way since 2006, and Veronica's mother is currently consulting a genetics specialist in search of more answers.

Recently Veronica attended a Bloomhill Cancer Care fundraising event, and she was thrilled to meet Raelene Boyle face-to-face – and Raelene was so touched to meet her. Veronica would be 100% flat-chested had it not been for the funding, and it was so important to her to convey her appreciation.

For all that she has been through, Veronica is still so optimistic, and a lover of life. 'I'm glad I listened to my red flag about the painful lump – I am cancer free!'

A final note...

What an incredible fighter you are, Veronica – I love your tenacity and your ability to keep going, despite everything.

Veronica's story speaks for itself. It reveals the bravery of a woman daring to choose to live a full life. However, I know Veronica well, and I know she has compared her journey to the journey of others (and probably still does – we are all guilty of this). I don't know how many times I've told her how incredible and amazing she is, and of the courage she must have had to say goodbye to her breasts. Veronica has had to dig deep to find herself and to know her worth and value as a woman, even without her breasts. If she can realise her value, you can realise yours!

Veronica also took the risk of allowing her nipples to be re-created from her very own flesh – that takes balls (pardon the pun)! Each of us has our own tolerance level for the various pains of life, and we don't have to minimise ours in order to enlarge someone else's. Conversely, you don't need to have experienced a high level of pain (like Veronica's) in order to find yourself. Sometimes we just need to realise who we are, and to recognise the strength and courage we have inside of us. We each have what we need to take us through the individual path of our life.

It may be that you or a loved one are facing cancer right now or, sadly, it may be that cancer is something you face in the future – unfortunately, statistics indicate that around one in every seven women is diagnosed with breast cancer by the age of 85 (not that I believe we should focus on negative statistics – in fact, I don't even like citing these statistics here, but we have to be in reality about the odds).

My advice is to listen to your body, and *not* to ignore any red flags. Know your body and take note of what it's telling you. Oh, and don't delay having that dreaded mammogram (hmm... speaking of which, I should get onto that!). However, remember, it was an ultrasound that picked up on Veronica's multiple lumps. She may not have been diagnosed with breast cancer, but her DCIS diagnosis and family history put her at risk and is why doctors made the horrific recommendation of a mastectomy. To educate yourself about breast cancer, check out organisations such as Cancer Council (cancer.org.au/about-cancer/types-of-cancer/breast-cancer) or Breast Cancer Network Australia (bcna.org.au).

There is so much wisdom to be gained from Veronica's story, even if you don't have a potentially serious illness. I'm sure that Veronica has had 'red flags' pop up in other areas of her life. I'm sure you could think of a few red flags you've seen (and either ignored or acted on) in your own life, whether it be in health, relationships, finances or career. I know I sure can. So often we women ignore red flags, but it's so important that we don't!

Has Veronica's story inspired you? I believe that every woman's life and story is an inspiration to someone else. You know, sometimes I read stories (especially the stories in this book), and I just stand in awe. While my own story may be different from others, I feel so INSPIRED – I believe that if she can do all of that, go through all of that and suffer through all of that, then... I'VE GOT THIS! I can do what I'm called to do in this life and I can achieve my life's vision. You know what? So can you! It's *your* choice to take certain actions when you see or hear red flags (just as Veronica chose to have her symptoms checked out), and I'm continually amazed at women who just keep on living, despite the challenges thrown up by their red flags!

On the flip side, though, I feel so sad for women who choose to nurture a chip on their shoulder. Women who allow the knockdowns to keep them down and who fall deeper and deeper into a spiral of depression. If this is you, I want to encourage you by assuring you that the red flags are sent for a *reason*. This book was written for you. You are my reason and I'm here to help you!

The first step – and sometimes the only step – needed is to connect, to reach out. As I mentioned in this book's Introduction, please do get in touch if you are facing a challenge in your life. Connect with me in any way that works for you, but please know that I am here for you. Veronica not only took notice of her red flags, she also chose her perspective and turned to her support network – and this got her through. It would be an honour for me to be part of your support network, too.

Real Women, Real Stories

a special message from...

VERONICA

JERRY MOORE

TWENTIETH-CENTURY ARRANGED MARRIAGE

Before we begin...

I first met Jerry through my Sydney-based business partner. She soon became my very special friend, confidant, cheerleader and mentor, and I am so grateful for that. However, would you believe that Jerry lives in Montana, and we are yet to meet in person? (Here's hoping I get to Montana for a book launch! Who wants to come?) We have met face-to-face via Zoom and Marco Polo – ah, the wonders of having an internet-based business partnership – and this technology has allowed us to form a deep bond. In life it's so important to have mentors who have walked the path before us, and I have so much love and respect for this lady. Jerry is in her 70s and is an entrepreneur running several successful businesses. She is so young at heart. It was a pleasure to invite Jerry to share some of her life wisdom with us, and I can't wait for you to read about her special love story.

Jerry's story

The year was 1966, and the world was being turned upside down by the Beatles, free love and drugs. OK, hands up – who remembers this era? I wasn't yet born! It was March, and Jerry was getting ready to start her third year of college. For this 19-year-old, the future shone bright with grandiose ideas of travelling the world, joining the navy or becoming a forest ranger. These thoughts had been born when Jerry worked a summer job at Grand Teton National Park in Wyoming. It was there that she worked on a dude ranch as the kitchen manager. That summer had been an education in itself.

AN EYE-OPENING SUMMER

Although she was from a big city, back then Jerry was not street smart. In fact, she was one of those girls who everyone thought was a 'prude'. Yep, she had no idea that high-school girls were having sex or doing drugs. That wasn't Jerry's way of living – she was a good Christian girl. However, the dude ranch was anything but Christian. Jerry met her first hippies, her first unmarried couple and her first lesbian, and she had her first taste of alcohol. She met a chef from Hungary and a child who killed a 30-year-old horse with a knife. You name it, she saw it. This place was totally decadent. I wonder if Jerry's parents really knew what this place was like?

Jerry's favourite ranch experience was horse riding. There were over 108 horses at the ranch, and as soon as work ended for the day, Jerry would jump on a horse and ride bareback. However, this wasn't the smartest idea. She was only 5ft 2in and rode a horse that was over 15 hands in height, so she had to have a stool nearby to mount up. Riding alone one day, she rounded a corner in the forest and came upon a mother bear and two cubs raiding an open garbage pit. The

Twentieth-Century Arranged Marriage

bear spooked her horse and off came Jerry, right in front of the mama bear. Fortunately, Jerry was able to gather herself, calm the horse and move away slowly, reins in hand, and find a tree stump to re-mount. Thankfully, Mama Bear was more interested in the garbage than in Jerry.

The chef at the dude ranch was from Hungary, and he had left his wife and children to suffer under his country's Russian invasion during the 1956 revolution. He bragged and laughed about having left his family. Occasionally he would get mad at the kitchen staff and threaten to rape each of them. This wouldn't (quite rightfully) be accepted these days, would it? Thankfully, his moods would pass but the staff were always wary around him.

Despite all of the eye-opening experiences at the ranch, Jerry was still a 'prude' at heart. She made it out alive and remained true to her beliefs and values. However, she now had her eyes wide open to the ways of the world. This education was instrumental in shaping her attitude towards life and in strengthening her convictions.

LET THE LOVE BEGIN

Jerry returned home from the ranch in September and waited for college to resume. It was during this time that her dad decided she needed to meet a young colleague of his called Richard. Jerry's family was middle-class, and her dad was working a second job as a part-time ambulance driver. Richard was a full-time policeman who was also working a second job as a part-time ambulance driver. Jerry and Richard both knew they were being set up by her dad, and they hit it off immediately. Richard was good-looking and had been working as an extra in TV commercials on the side. He was also ambitious and very disciplined, with police work being his passion.

So, in the week before school was to due to re-start, the phone monopolised Jerry's nights. She would spend hours talking with Richard about everything imaginable, and she felt herself falling in love. Whenever the phone rang she felt a thrill. She also went out with Richard on a couple of dinner dates and to the movies. Back then, girls didn't pay for anything, men opened doors for them and courteousness was a given. Life was simpler. Jerry's dad was thrilled, of course, that he'd found for her someone decent and who had a great work ethic. Jerry's mum was OK with her decision to date and never really said much either way.

Richard arranged to drive Jerry back to college, and it was a 60-mile trip. Once they arrived, he took her to dinner and told her all about his life and gave her a crazy sob story about girls not wanting to date cops. (Looking back, Jerry realises this wasn't true because Richard had women chasing him constantly – but that was to end shortly!) Little did Richard know that Jerry loved cops. As a teenager, she had worked for three summers at the Kansas City Missouri Police Department and, to top it off, Jerry's mother worked for the chief of police. So even if other girls didn't want to date him, Jerry sure did. That evening ended all too soon, with Richard driving back to Kansas City and Jerry heading to her dorm.

WHEN YOU KNOW, YOU KNOW

Once back at her dorm, Jerry announced to her three roommates that she was quitting college and going home to get married. Jerry says, 'I knew! I knew that Richard was the ONE'. She had been dating college boys for two years – she had been serious about some, but others were just 'yuck'. Jerry knew what she wanted and what she didn't want. She called her mother and told her the news. Jerry's mother was stunned. She was unhappy with her decision and thought that she should complete her degree in recreation, especially because she was so close to finishing. This career was also something new in the workforce and it promised travel and loads of excitement. However, her mother agreed that if this was what Jerry wanted then she needed to come home.

The next morning, Richard called Jerry's mother to tell her that Jerry had made it back to college on time. Her mother briskly announced that Jerry was quitting college and getting married. He said, 'Who is she marrying?' She said, 'You'. Jerry's mother was sure shock had set in for Richard because the subject had never been discussed. Jerry didn't know until later that Richard had been engaged to another girl when they met; however, he had ended it immediately when he realised that Jerry would be 'the one'. Jerry definitely trusted her intuition: 'He was exactly what I was looking for in a husband. I knew he was the one and never doubted it'.

Despite this, Richard didn't propose until two months later. Why? Well, Jerry says, 'I loved the mountains, and wanted to go back to Wyoming to live and work on the dude ranch once we'd married. There were no mountains in the big city where I was from'. Unfortunately, Richard wanted to stay put and continue being a cop, and he wouldn't propose until he knew that Jerry would be OK with staying in Kansas. He wasn't going to move. He was an only child and was extremely close to his parents. His parents weren't really happy that Richard had become serious about the crazy girl he had just met. So, Jerry decided to give up her hopes of living in the mountains of Wyoming. When she agreed to staying in the city, Richard officially proposed, and they married soon after.

Jerry describes Richard as a decisive person: he was smart, hardworking, bold, protective and moral, had absolute common sense and, as mentioned before, was extremely

Her mother briskly announced that Jerry was quitting college and getting married.
He said, 'Who is she marrying?'
She said, 'You'.

Twentieth-Century Arranged Marriage

attractive (that may have had something to do with her choice – wink, wink) – although she feels that a potential husband's appearance was low on her priority list. Having said that, Jerry tells us, 'He could have been Chuck Norris' twin'. Jerry wasn't looking for a husband, but everything in her being told her that this was the right person. 'I know God was watching out for me,' Jerry says. Jerry and Richard were married three months after they met. She was 20 and he was 24. The wedding was very simple and it was the very first wedding she had ever been to. That was 52 years ago.

ON THE SAME PAGE

For the first three years of their married life, Jerry says Richard was a macho non-believing man, who often threw her Bible in the trash. She says now, 'It's a wonder God didn't strike him dead'. Mind you, that's not something God would do! Richard's heart was truly in his job as a policeman, but that profession was one of brotherhood, foul language and working with unsavoury people. Richard dealt in the dirt of the world. It was a dangerous job, one in which his life was at risk every day. Jerry knew that if Richard was killed on the job, she'd be devastated to lose the love of her life – however, she took some comfort in knowing that she would have financial security from insurance coverage and could start over. She says, 'I wasn't one of those worrywarts who constantly thought about the "what ifs" in life'. How good would it be to have this mindset? So often we focus on worrying about all the negatives of life.

Jerry lovingly tells us that, during their third year of marriage, 'Because of God's mercy and grace, Richard accepted the Lord Jesus Christ as his saviour'. In the fourth year, God called Richard to preach and be a pastor at a church. This changed their married life forever because they were both now bonded in the Lord. She admits they have sometimes had growing pains since that time, but they have always been on the same page of life.

Jerry and Richard have moved all over the United States, moving 41 times in 52 years. (Wow!) Jerry has friends all over the country, and loved moving to new areas where new friends could be made and customs learned. Some of their moves were because of business, some were because of church, and some were just for fun. Their children gathered more air miles than most people will ever have. They treasured those years, although their children (Patrick and Meredith) sometimes wondered where home really was!

THE FOUNDATIONS

Jerry and Richard's married life is built on three main foundations. These were instilled in her at a young age through her family's strong religious beliefs. They are:

1. **Love** – love others unconditionally
2. **Give** – a wife gives 90% into a marriage and a husband gives 10%
3. **Talk** – talk to each other, with no holding back

With these foundations, and their Christian beliefs and values, Richard has always valued Jerry's opinion, loved her unconditionally and treated her as his equal. Jerry attributes the success of their 52-year marriage to the love and support they have always given each other. She is also so thankful to her grandmother, who had prayed that Jerry would find Mr Right, and to her dad, who knew what she really needed – Richard.

In 1975, one of their moves took them to the mountains of Montana. Her heart had longed for mountains, and Montana (described as huge, wide and handsome) is the largest Rocky

Twentieth-Century Arranged Marriage

Mountain state in the United States. Jerry had stayed true to her path of marrying the man she knew was right for her, while patiently waiting for her beloved Rocky Mountains. Jerry's unwavering faith had brought those two loves into her life.

A final note...

Who loves a good love story? I know for sure there are many other stories that Jerry could also have shared from the past 52 years but, alas, we only have one chapter. In reflecting on her special love story, I would say that having a praying grandmother, mother or father (or friend, for that matter) is to be treasured above all else, no matter what your beliefs might be. Imagine having someone pray that your life partner would be exactly who you'd need?

As I mentioned in the introduction to this chapter, I've only communicated with Jerry in an online setting, but as my business partner and friend I've grown to love and value the wisdom of her life. There may be some who question the value of the three main foundations on which Jerry's marriage is built. We may judge and say, 'Well, that was then, but this is now – times and values have changed'. However, let's wait a minute before we brush over these points. Let's dive a bit deeper:

1. **Love** – unconditional love needs to underpin any relationship that we value. Unconditional love is a choice. It is love that is based on who a person is and not on what they do. You can choose to take the higher road, no matter what. Many times in this fast-paced world we love based on the *actions*

of a person and how they make us feel, only loving in return for what they can do for us – that is not unconditional love!

2. **Give** – 'a wife gives 90% into a marriage and a husband gives 10%'. WHAT are you saying, Jerry? Why do I have to give 90%?!

    The way I see it, no one is stopping your man from giving more than 10%. In fact, men and women should be giving 100% to each other – can you imagine the types of marriages and relationships we would have if we did this? My motto is 'live to give to change lives', and this starts in the home. More often than not women do give, and we keep giving... but are we giving the other person what they need? Or are we giving what is easy to give or what we want to give?

    The quality of what we give each other is key here. It's important to become selfless and to know that the more we give without expectation, the more we will receive (even if it's not from your husband/partner/parent/children). Adopting an attitude of 'living to give' with a generous heart is what matters in every relationship. Putting others first makes all the difference. Does that mean, though, that you give up on personal self-care? No! Not at all. In fact, you should be doing the opposite. To be able to give and be focused on others we need to fuel ourselves first. To take this conversation further, I invite you to join my 'Building Success Habits for Active Women' group. Simply head here and ask to join: facebook.com/groups/BuildingSuccessHabits.

3. **Talk** – 'talk to each other, with no holding back'. Good communication is the foundation of healthy relationships. I've heard so many women say

Twentieth-Century Arranged Marriage

that they don't talk to their husbands or partners about things – they say, 'What's the point?' I've occasionally thought this, as well! Well, 'the point' is that if you want to know something, resolve something or understand something it's so important to make the time to communicate. If you don't know how to approach things, invest in a communication course. Don't make excuses for not talking – create reasons to talk and have those potentially not-so-fun conversations!

Communication is one of my favourite topics, because it really is a two-way street – when you communicate you are talking *and* listening, in order to understand. It's not a complex subject but there is definitely a lot more to it than most people realise. I'm so glad Jerry included it as one of the foundations of her marriage because it is essential for good relationships and for life in general.

You know, I truly stand in awe of women (and men) who have had such long marriages – WOW, 52 years for Jerry and Richard! I hope and pray that one day I'll also be able to say I've been married that long.

But how about you? Where is your love story taking you?

In life you know to expect the unexpected, and that there will be challenges to overcome. You also know there will be opportunities. So it is, too, with your love story... every day and in every relationship, you have the opportunity to love, to give and to talk. Loving communication is key. I hope that Jerry's love story has washed over you with fresh inspiration for your life!

Real Women, Real Stories

a special message from...

JERRY

NORMA IRONSIDE

HE GIVETH MORE GRACE

Before we begin...

How does one introduce their mother within the pages of a book? (I have never had this particular experience before!) As I mentioned in the 'A Message from Jennifer' chapter at the beginning of this book, I start each story by sharing how I met the woman featured in that particular story. So, how did I meet Norma Ironside? Well, in the womb! She is my amazing mother and my hero. She is also a born and bred Aussie girl, raised on a cane farm in Bundaberg, Queensland. This is where she completed her schooling and undertook four years of general nursing. Mum then relocated to Tasmania, specialising in midwifery. At the age of 23 she married her only love, David, and enjoyed raising their four children – three boys and a girl. I'm honoured to share with you just a portion of my mum's story, and I know that it will inspire you and challenge you. Her life has never been the same since she went through the amazing experience you'll be reading about – it was seriously life-changing. She demonstrates the importance of being open-minded and growing as a woman by embracing challenging opportunities and getting out of your comfort zone. She really does model how to be a woman of substance, an audacious woman who dares to pursue her calling! (I hope you don't mind, but because she is my mum we'll refer to her as such throughout the story.)

Norma's story

It was a beautiful spring morning in mid-September of 1988 when the phone rang. 'I wonder who it could be?' Mum thought. It was her husband, David (my dad), with an interesting proposal.

'How would you feel about going to Malawi, Africa?' he said. 'What?' Mum said. She had never heard of the place! (Malawi is a small landlocked country in south-east Africa, and was originally known as Nyasaland.) However, before they knew it, they – Dad, Mum and seven-year-old Nathan (my brother) – were packed up and on their way to Malawi, leaving only their furniture behind. Mum remembers sitting on the plane as it was about to leave the tarmac at Maroochydore airport, gazing anxiously out the window and thinking, 'What an earth are we getting ourselves into?'

They were shocked when they arrived. Things were so different! You couldn't begin to imagine details such as the somewhat inefficient customs process, the clean but hot airport, the tidy streets, the change of culture, the different people, the unpleasant aroma... everything they knew to be normal had been left behind. They were now in a foreign land.

THE ADVENTURE BEGINS

A representative from the Malawi Ministry of Agriculture met them at the airport, and as they were driven to their motel they noticed the scaffolding against some buildings was made of mere bamboo. On the drive they were informed of the seriousness of that particular day, as it was a national holiday. There would be no welcome party or celebrations, as frivolity was not permitted. It was 3 March, Martyrs' Day, a day for honouring military and political heroes. People were to be quiet and sombre for the entire day, shops were closed and people weren't to go anywhere. They were told to contain their excitement because it would be dishonouring to the nation. If expatriates such as Mum and Dad disobeyed these laws in any way, they could be given three days to leave the country. 'It was very strange!' Mum says. Being told by the government what she could and couldn't wear and when they could celebrate was all part of their interesting introduction to Malawi, and so it was that their amazing, life-changing 5½-year adventure had begun.

Over the coming days and weeks they were to discover that Malawi had beautiful countryside with rolling plains of tea, coffee, tobacco and macadamia plantations. Dad had been contracted as a macadamia specialist with the Malawian government, and although the government was meant to have arranged accommodation for the family, it hadn't happened in time for their arrival. Fortunately, a macadamia grower opened his home for them to stay in for two weeks, and after that they moved to a very large house on a coffee and tea estate that also grew macadamias.

What an experience.

The estate was some two hours' drive from the closest town and was deep in the heart of the country. Mum had to find and employ a 'houseboy' (a male domestic worker), gardener and night-watchman, as this was a requirement for white folk working in Malawi. This is not easy when you can't speak the language! Their stay at the coffee and tea estate was only temporary, because the government was arranging a house for them on the research station. Unfortunately, the process of finding them a house was very slow and took several months, meaning that Nathan had to go to boarding school. This disappointed Mum and Dad greatly because they had been promised that this situation wouldn't happen... however, Nathan adjusted quickly and fitted in well, playing with expat and local children and quickly learning the language.

A BAPTISM OF FIRE

Eventually they moved to Bvumbwe Research Station and had a house of their own. When they first moved in there were no curtains or mats. Most importantly, there were also no mosquito nets – and these were a necessity because malaria is a serious condition. They were attacked by mosquitoes a couple of times. As was the case at the coffee and tea estate, they also employed staff. Here they had the help of a house girl, who did most of the work; a garden boy, who ensured they had a flourishing garden; and a night-watchman.

It was crucial to have a watchman because it was common for homes to be robbed. They were robbed three times, including one night waking to crashing noises beside the bedroom window and seeing robbers leap out with all of Dad's expensive cameras, lenses and a video camera, and their clothing, shoes and bags. On another occasion robbers entered through the back door when the family wasn't home, and took out batches of belongings through the front door. Mum and Dad arrived home in the middle of the robbery. Dad ended up chasing one of the men down the road, with the man clutching Nathan's toys in his arms. They never did get back any of their belongings – they just had to adopt an attitude of 'clearly they needed them more', because often robbers would sell the goods for money.

However, being settled on the research station enabled Nathan to become a day student, and this was most important to them. Having a seven-year-old going to boarding school in a foreign country was a huge safety concern. Having said that, Nathan is forever grateful for his years in Malawi. His experience of Malawian culture and its way of life made a real impact on him. Living in Africa throughout his formative years allowed him to develop beyond his years. He deeply appreciates having had the opportunity to learn how to adapt to, and enjoy, another culture. He is now a bilingual artist, producer and pastor, and he is married to a beautiful Spanish girl called Mary. Nathan and Mary live in Colombia with their two children, Hannah and Joshua.

STRUGGLES ACROSS THE MILES

In the beginning, life in Malawi was not easy. They experienced culture shock. They were isolated and without a car. They were homesick for their other children and for their friends. Then came news about the break-up of my first marriage. It was difficult to hear that news, to say the least. They couldn't ring me because phone lines were usually unavailable. Mum says, 'The news came to us not through my daughter Jennifer, but from her then-husband, and it was such a shock! I was very upset'. Yes, it was a shock because I had hidden my problems from them before they left for Africa – I hadn't wanted them to worry about me. She took herself on long walks through the coffee plantation and shed many tears. Mum had long had a belief and trust in God, and at this time she turned to that belief for support. This enabled her to receive His comfort to her heart. She had a revelation of God's great love, and was able to forgive me and my then-husband. Never before had she encountered a situation like this with anyone close to her heart, and especially not with her children.

Throughout her life, Mum (and Dad) had met with many couples struggling in their marriages, but this was different. 'How could this have happened to my daughter?' she thought. 'What did I miss with this?' She had been able to help so many others to overcome their challenges, yet she had not been able to make the same difference in the life of her daughter. This was totally out of her hands. Mum could only pray, and trust that someone else and God would be there to help me – and they were. Mind you, I was going through a stage of being headstrong and rebellious about everything. Clearly, this situation was too sensitive and we were too far away from each other, but eventually Mum was able to talk with me. Divorce was as foreign a subject for my family as was their foreign home in Malawi, so it was never something I wanted to bring up with my mum – that's for sure!

ADJUSTING TO A NEW LIFE

Despite the turmoil happening back home in Australia, and the anguish Mum and Dad felt about it, their new life in Malawi went on.

Dad continued to fulfil his contract with the Malawian government. This allowed Mum time to undertake voluntary work with the local women, to share their experiences and to learn a little more about their culture. Malawian women are unique. They love to look beautiful and dress up – Mum never ceased to be amazed at their ability to do this, given their lack of resources. Speaking of resources, shopping was different to how it was in Australia. There was only one supermarket and you didn't have a choice of brands. Some products – particularly imported products – were very expensive. The markets were truly amazing. Every week they visited them to obtain fresh vegetables, meat and fish. The smell and flies were something else – enough to make you want to vomit (some people avoided them completely)! However, you were able to get all that was necessary, and it was cheap. Many of the market entrances were lined with fish laying on sheets covering the ground. Mum says, 'One market even had rows of chooks, with their heads and feet boiled, and yellow in colour, just sitting there on the ground looking at you while you walked past'. Any wonder Mum, Dad and Nathan felt ill!

Malawi is known for its belief in Christianity, and Mum and Dad were delighted to join a local church. Malawi is also known as the 'Warm Heart of Africa', and that is true. The women Mum encountered were warm-hearted and humble. 'I loved them,' Mum says. 'I had the joy of ministering to them, encouraging them and helping them to grow in their faith and knowledge of God.'

Mum says, 'I developed some beautiful friendships during my time there, and some 25 years later I still have contact with many of the women'. However, Mum couldn't get over the number of women who lived with a death sentence hanging over their heads because their husbands had contracted HIV. She was shocked, and couldn't imagine coping with this, but she had the privilege of supporting them and loving them through this horrific ordeal. Unfortunately, many of those beautiful women did contract HIV.

SPREADING HOPE

The time Mum spent travelling throughout Africa, especially in the south and central-east parts, was interesting for her. She had become the international director for Women's Aglow Fellowship (now known as Aglow International), an inspiring Christian women's organisation. This role required her to travel and work in seven different nations. She encountered many challenges, from being held up, to squatting to go to the toilet on the side of the road, to losing passports and losing luggage (due to its non-arrival). She became very well known for her inspiring speaking ability, teaching women of all ages of the love of God and how to live with grace and dignity regardless of their circumstances. Those teachings were put to the test many times throughout Mum's own life, and certainly when she faced hair-raising situations in a country that was foreign to her.

One such experience that comes to her mind is when she and a group of ladies had travelled across the Zambian border and into Zaire. They were travelling to a meeting to speak and their car was pulled off the road by the military police, with them being ordered out of the car with guns to their heads. The police searched their luggage but found nothing, so they were allowed to proceed. Although this was a harrowing experience, they had an amazing sense of peace, knowing they were on their journey with the purpose of encouraging women. Once in Zaire they were taken to a Catholic monastery for safety, as they had arrived in the middle of a civil war. However, even in those circumstances they felt privileged to have the opportunity to share with the women who came to hear their inspiring messages of hope.

You know the saying 'the apple doesn't fall far from the tree'? Well, as I write Mum's story with her, tears well up in my eyes when I realise that I didn't know a lot about what

Although this was a harrowing experience, they had an amazing sense of peace, knowing they were on their journey with the purpose of encouraging women.

she was experiencing at that time in her life. I had little to no knowledge of some of the dangerous situations she was in, or of the influence she was having in this foreign country. I heard the stories on her return, but even then I didn't fully appreciate the depth or the importance of what it meant to her. Nor did I understand how fulfilling it is to truly know your life purpose. When you look outside of yourself and become others-focused, you see life differently. Your life feels complete, and your feeling of purpose enables you to push through challenges. If you feel as though there's something missing in your life, perhaps not knowing your life's purpose means there is a question mark hanging above your head.

Two- and three-day conferences were a common feature of the work Mum and her group did while in Africa. These conferences were held not just in Malawi, but in Zimbabwe and Zambia. Women came from all over the continent and at great expense. They overcame many challenges to be there so that they could be inspired and encouraged – practically (such as by sharing household and mothering skills) and spiritually (such as by sharing biblical principles).

TIME TO SAY GOODBYE

While there had been so many cultural differences and adjustments to make, personally and as a family, Mum says, 'It was such a joy to bring our open-home policy and hospitable family culture to these beautiful people'. With a picnic lunch in hand they often gathered up friends and David's work colleagues and headed to spectacular Lake Malawi, a two-hour drive from their home. Nathan had made some good friends with expatriate families through school, and they also joined them. Spending time boating became one of the great pleasures of their time in Malawi.

After 5½ years, Dad's contract was coming to an end and all Mum could say was, 'David, is there something else you can do so we can stay here? Is there another contract you could apply for?' Malawi had become home for her, despite all the challenges of adapting to the culture of a developing nation. She had become increasingly fulfilled by her work of helping women, especially through her role with Women's Aglow. Mum did not want to pack up and say goodbye to her adopted country and friends. There were so many farewells; so many celebrations to be had. One of the beautiful Malawian women referred to Mum as her mother, mentor and friend and they remain in contact even to this day.

'My heart is still full of love for that beautiful country and its people,' Mum says, with a lump in her throat. 'Many fond memories remain, along with the scary ones.' Mum would love to return for a visit, having only been able to return three times in the past 25 years. 'Much may have changed but, oh, how I'd love to see the country that I called home just once more,' she says.

'HELLO' TO ANOTHER CULTURE

Some years after their return to Australia, Mum had the opportunity to share with the Aboriginal women of Katherine, in Australia's Northern Territory. My parents were pastors of a church for six years, and it was a very different experience from that of Africa. African women were keen to progress and improve themselves whereas Aboriginal women were content with their lot. Unique and wonderful in their own way.

Women all around the world face the same challenges, no matter what their culture. They all have similar issues and frustrations. Many face relationship concerns while others have financial difficulties. Yet others have health problems. 'We are all real women with a real story,' says Mum, 'all at different stages of life'. Part of real life can also involve experiencing ill health...

HEALTH CHALLENGES

For over 60 years Mum enjoyed good health. She was strong and vibrant and able to enjoy life, having never been in hospital since giving birth to Nathan some 37 years prior. However, on the verge of turning 79 she had a stroke. She spent a few days in hospital, including her 79th birthday.

Everything down the right side of her body was affected, from walking to writing. She was also not able to think clearly. Mum's memory was not impacted, although at times she had difficulty finding the right words to express herself. Thankfully, Dad called for me to come, and I was with them throughout the hospital and rehab experience and until after Mum arrived home. 'Jennifer was a great help to us,' she says. 'She prepared many frozen meals, tidied up, did washing, and spent time teaching her dad new household tricks while I was in recovery.' Another new experience was having me boss them around, but we all laughed and joked – this helped take away the seriousness of what everyone was going through. I was actually rather obsessed with making sure that Mum was doing her rehab exercises, and that Dad was going to look after Mum. She has always been my rock, and still is, but I became very aware that the roles were slowly changing and that I needed to be the rock for both of my parents. However, I'm grateful that Mum and Dad had a laugh and made light of some of my demands!

After her stroke, Mum's main frustration was with walking. The fact that she needed a hip and knee replacement didn't help. She had difficulty getting up and down and had constant pain. Mum believes that God can heal and strengthen her ligaments. It's been more than two years since her stroke, and on occasion she still experiences some pain and discomfort. However, there has been much improvement, and for this she is very thankful.

MUM'S MESSAGE FOR YOU

Mum's love and passion for helping women, and for being an amazing wife and mother, has never waned in all of her 80 years. She has given her children, grandchildren and great-grandchildren that amazing legacy to follow. Mum would like to leave you with this biblical passage, which is a mantra for her life:

> 'Trust God from the bottom of your heart;
> don't try to figure out everything on your own.
> Listen for God's voice in everything you do,
> everywhere you go;
> He's the one who will keep you on track.
> Don't assume that you know it all...
> (Bible Proverbs 3:5-6)

And remember – with Him all things are possible!

A final note...

If I can be only half the woman my mother is, I'll feel accomplished. There are so many untold stories and details from her life, and I hope one day to write them for her. My mother has the most amazing qualities. She truly is the epitome of a woman of substance! My mother has always put OTHERS first and is entirely focused on doing this.

What coaching tips could I possibly leave you with after thinking about my mum's story?

You know, regardless of what you believe about spiritual matters, when it comes to God there's one thing I know and have learned to do. That is – trust God!

Do I always trust Him perfectly? No, I don't, but when I do, when I truly give Him all my concerns to handle, it takes the pressure off and I can just relax and live my best life! Many people ask where my positivity comes from. Well, this is where – my beliefs and trust in God and in the amazing mum who 'lives to give'.

If you want to create a fulfilling life, just as my mum has done, live a life of purpose. Have a vision and put others at the centre. Everything else will be taken care of. Allow yourself to live and enjoy your life, regardless of the challenges. When you know your purpose, you will succeed – and you will get through anything.

He Giveth More Grace

a special message from...

NORMA

Some Final Words

I have learnt so much from each and every one of these stories. I have been blown away by each woman's tenacity, and by the audacity she had to look her real-life challenges in the face and yet choose to live a bigger life.

You also have the opportunity to choose to live a full life. Few people understand that they have the power of choice – they allow the negatives of life to dictate their futures.

So, how can you live a full life? The answer is different for everyone, but to get the ball rolling, I invite you to grab a journal (available from my website) and to jot down the first thoughts that enter your mind when you read the following questions:

- Who am I?
- What is my purpose?
- What are my dreams? Who will be affected if they are achieved (or if they're not)?
- What impact do I want to have?
- What is my life vision?

If you begin this exercise but then think, 'Jen, my mind went blank,' then try writing as though you are having a private conversation with me. Doing this will soon reveal the underlying answers, and more. Alternatively, simply ask yourself this question: 'What do I want?'

Real Women, Real Stories

The benefits are vast when you ponder these questions – they bring clarity, help identify your greater purpose, remind you of your connection to others and motivate you to take action.

Life's challenges and opportunities never end. There will always be something new to learn, new experiences to be had, and new opportunities to give to others. We are ever-evolving in this life, and we should make it our mission to transform, just a little, each and every day. We should be different today from who we were yesterday, regardless of the type of journey we are on. The core of you is perfect in every way and makes you 'you', and your evolution serves to strip away the pain and beliefs that were thrust upon you from conception. In the midst of turmoil – or even of celebration – we so often forget that we have the opportunity, right in that moment, to learn and grow and see the positives that can come from the situation at hand. Every action you take today creates your future, your *real story*.

While my heartfelt intention with this book was to reach into your life and let you know that you are not alone, I also want to inspire you to take action in your life. I encourage you to re-read the stories from this book that resonate with you the most. Take the lessons and messages from those stories and commit to taking one life-changing action today and every day until it becomes routine (a great first goal is to do this twice a day). Then choose another action and repeat. By working together, we can ensure that you LIVE YOUR BEST LIFE NOW.

Real woman – **you** are the writer of your story!

Much love to you (and do reach out and connect with me)...

Jen xox

Acknowledgements

Goodness, where do I start? To be honest, I didn't ever think I'd be sitting here typing this for my very first book! If it wasn't for my faith in God and for each and every person in my life – from the past and in the present – and for you, the reader... well, simply put, we wouldn't be here!

Within this book I've been honoured to share the stories of some remarkable, everyday real women from around the globe. To each of my contributors, I say thank you. Your precious story has brought life to the vision of this book. I'm so grateful to each one of you for being vulnerable and real. You trusted me to present your story to the world so that it could impact the lives of others. Thank you so much. Special thanks goes to Lynda Brook, who asked me week after week, 'How is the book going? Have you started yet, Jen?' Lynda, you inspired me to my very core and I'm so grateful that you did.

To the beautiful Joanne Newell of Rich Life By Design, who has believed in my vision right from the start – even when I doubted that I had 'my beautiful book' (as she called it) within me. Thank you for your professionalism, integrity and publishing skills. We would never have made it otherwise, especially with my one-fingered typing skills! You are so much more than a publishing consultant; thank you to your team, from the bottom of my heart. You all chose to know me better than I sometimes know myself.

Real Women, Real Stories

We all have a mother, right? Well, my mum surpasses them all (in my opinion ☺). Thanks, Mum, for the life you live and for being a woman of substance. You showed me that I could open doors to a world of opportunity, hope and destiny. You've created an amazing legacy, and my desire is to do you proud at every turn. Thank you for leading and guiding me throughout my life, even when I didn't want to be!

Daughters are such a blessing – hugs and thanks to you, Rochelle, my daughter. Thank you for being by my side and willingly taking off your mask with me.

And to all of you, my readers – thank you for your reviews and recommendations. I know that as you apply the wisdom and tips from this book's stories you will LIVE YOUR BEST LIFE NOW.

Love always, with a forever grateful heart...

PS Thanks also to Jen Griswold, author of *Mission Entrepreneur* and my Rodan + Fields business partner – Jen, your life, leadership example and personal and professional trainings have expanded my belief and staying power. Because of you, I consistently take action and celebrate daily successes.

PPS This list could go on! However, my publisher is counting the words ☺.

About Jennifer

Jennifer Ironside has failed. A LOT. Yep, she's just your regular, all-Aussie mum, gran, daughter, sister and friend, and she's stumbled and tripped more times than she cares to remember.

If it wasn't for her stubbornness and fierce independence, she wouldn't have found herself in hot water quite so often. Yet it's those very traits that are now being used for good in her life, and in the lives of others.

A dynamic, down-to-earth natural leader with a big heart, Jennifer has held management and leadership positions *and* been a single mum. She now lives her purpose by inspiring women around the world to imagine and deliberately create an authentic life. She knows it's possible to overcome crippling adversity, and to make the choice to transform your life – after all, she's done just that with her own life!

When she's not helping other women, she loves smelling the roses (literally), indulging in Thai food (bring on the chilli), sipping sweet red wine (Brown Brothers, thank you very much), watching movies (have you seen *A Star Is Born*?) and, best of all, spending time with her beautiful family (including her GlamBabies (grandbabies) Harper, Carson, Zaine and Alora).

To discover more about this inspiring woman and all she has to offer, head to jenniferironside.com.

More than a Vision

IF THIS BOOK HAS LIT A FIRE WITHIN YOUR SOUL, AND YOU KNOW YOU'RE READY TO MOVE YOUR LIFE FROM 'UNINSPIRED' TO 'UNSTOPPABLE', JENNIFER IS HERE TO HELP.

More than a Vision is Jennifer's unique program giving you the space to uncover your wildest dreams... and holding your hand while you bring those dreams to life.

IT'S THE PERFECT BLEND OF DREAMING AND DOING!

Life isn't meant to be mediocre or filled with pain and suffering – it's YOUR time to create an inspiring new vision.

Head to:

MORETHANAVISION.COM

for all the details.

Review Request

Dear Reader

What have you loved most about *Real Women, Real Stories*? Do you have a favourite story?

 I would love to hear how my story and the stories of my contributors have helped you see your situation with fresh eyes. Are you going to live your life differently because of this book?

 I would appreciate it if you could share your thoughts with others by leaving a review. Your review may lead another woman to find the loving inspiration that (I hope!) you have found here.

 To leave a review simply go to the review section on the Amazon page for *Real Women, Real Stories*. Click on the big button that says 'Write a customer review' and enter your star rating and written review.

 Thank you so much…

PS It would mean the world to me to see you enjoying this book – please do share a photo of yourself with the book (and your thoughts and takeaways) on Facebook, and tag me using @GlobalTransformationCoach.

www.ingramcontent.com/pod-product-compliance
Lightning Source LLC
Chambersburg PA
CBHW050306010526
44107CB00055B/2125